AF609477

# BIHAR

## A STATE STUDY GUIDE

BRIJESH SINHA

*Published by*

**Hawk Press**
4836/24, Ansari Road, Daryaganj
New Delhi – 110 002
Phones: 91-11-23278618, 91-11-43667199
E-mail: thehawkpress@gmail.com
www.thehawkpress.com


ISBN: 978-93-88318-68-6

# Preface

Bihar is an Indian state considered to be a part of Eastern as well as Northern India. It is the thirteen-largest Indian state, with an area of 94,163 km (36,357 sq mi). As the third-largest state by population, it is contiguous with Uttar Pradesh to its west, Nepal to the north, the northern part of West Bengal to the east, with Jharkhand to the south. The Bihar plain is split by the river Ganges which flows from west to east. Bihar is an amalgamation of three distinct regions: Magadh, Mithila, and Bhojpur.

On 15 November 2000, southern Bihar was ceded to form the new state of Jharkhand. Only 11.3% of the population of Bihar lives in urban areas, which is the lowest in India after Himachal Pradesh. Additionally, almost 58% of Biharis are below the age of 25, giving Bihar the highest proportion of young people of any Indian state.

In ancient and classical India, the area that is now Bihar was considered a centre of power, learning, and culture. From Magadha arose India's first empire, the Maurya empire, as well as one of the world's most widely adhered-to religions, Buddhism. Magadha empires, notably under the Maurya and Gupta dynasties, unified large parts of South Asia under a central rule. Another region of Bihar is Mithila which was an early centre of Brahmanical learning and the centre of the Videha kingdom.

Buddhism in Magadha went into decline due to the invasion of Muhammad bin Bakhtiyar Khalji, during which many of the viharas and the famed universities of Nalanda and Vikramashila were destroyed. It was claimed that thousands of Buddhist monks were massacred during the 12th century. D. N. Jha suggests, instead, that these incidents were the result of Buddhist-

Brahmin skirmishes in a fight for supremacy. In 1540, the great Pathan chieftain, Sher Shah Suri, from Sasaram, took northern India from the Mughals, defeating the Mughal army of Emperor Humayun. Sher Shah declared Delhi his capital.

Since the late 1970s, Bihar has lagged far behind other Indian states in terms of social and economic development. Many economists and social scientists claim that this is a direct result of the policies of the central government, such as the Freight equalisation policy, its apathy towards Bihar, lack of Bihari sub-nationalism, and the Permanent Settlementof 1793 by the British East India Company. The state government has, however, made significant strides in developing the state. Improved governance has led to an economic revival in the state through increased investment in infrastructure, better health care facilities, greater emphasis on education, and a reduction in crime and corruption.

This is a reference book. All the matter is just compiled and edited in nature, taken from the various sources which are in public domain.

The book is of great importance for the scholars, researchers, students, teachers and historians as well pertaining to this sphere.

—*Editor*

# ABOUT THE BOOK

Bihar, the ancient land of Buddha, has witnessed golden period of Indian history. It is the same land where the seeds of the first republic were sown and which cultivated the first crop of democracy. Such fertile is the soil that has given birth to innumerous intellectuals which spread the light of knowledge and wisdom not only in the country but in the whole world. The state has its capital at Patna, which is situated on the bank of the holy river Ganga. For its geographical location, natural beauty, mythological and historical importance, Bihar feels proud of the assets it has been gifted by time. And for its moral contributions in the fields of arts-literature and religion and spiritualism, it knows no competitors centuries old stories related to this land are told even today. The state is the same kingdom, which once upon a time ruled the country as well as the neighbouring countries . Many great rulers have lived here and it fills us with a sense of pride when we think of Bihar as the 'Karmabhumi' of Buddha and Mahavir. Bihar, to liven up the glorious tale of which land, words fall short. The state as it is today has been shaped from its partition from the province of Bengal and most recently after the separation of the tribal southern region now called Jharkhand. The book is of great importance for the scholars, researchers, students, teachers and historians as well pertaining to this sphere.

# Contents

# 1

# State at a Glance

Bihar is an Indian state considered to be a part of Eastern as well as Northern India. It is the thirteen-largest Indian state, with an area of 94,163 km (36,357 sq mi). As the third-largest state by population, it is contiguous with Uttar Pradesh to its west, Nepal to the north, the northern part of West Bengal to the east, with Jharkhand to the south. The Bihar plain is split by the river Ganges which flows from west to east. Bihar is an amalgamation of three distinct regions: Magadh, Mithila, and Bhojpur.

On 15 November 2000, southern Bihar was ceded to form the new state of Jharkhand. Only 11.3% of the population of Bihar lives in urban areas, which is the lowest in India after Himachal Pradesh. Additionally, almost 58% of Biharis are below the age of 25, giving Bihar the highest proportion of young people of any Indian state.

In ancient and classical India, the area that is now Bihar was considered a centre of power, learning, and culture. From Magadha arose India's first empire, the Maurya empire, as well as one of the world's most widely adhered-to religions, Buddhism. Magadha empires, notably under the Maurya and Gupta dynasties, unified large parts of South Asia under a central rule. Another region of Bihar is Mithila which was an early centre of Brahmanical learning and the centre of the Videha kingdom.

Since the late 1970s, Bihar has lagged far behind other Indian states in terms of social and economic development. Many economists and social scientists claim that this is a direct result of the policies of the central government, such as the Freight equalisation policy, its apathy towards Bihar, lack of Bihari sub-nationalism, and the Permanent Settlementof 1793 by the British East India Company.

The state government has, however, made significant strides in developing the state. Improved governance has led to an economic revival in the state through increased investment in infrastructure, better health care facilities, greater emphasis on education, and a reduction in crime and corruption.

## ETYMOLOGY

The name *Bihar* is derived from the Sanskrit and Pali word, *Vihâra*, meaning "abode". The region roughly encompassing the present state was dotted with Buddhist vihara, the abodes of Buddhist monks in the ancient and medieval periods. Medieval writer Minhaj al-Siraj Juzjani records in the *Tabakat-i-Nasiri* that in 1198, Bakhtiyar Khalji committed a massacre in a town now known as Bihar Sharif, about 70 km away from Bodh Gaya.

## HISTORY

### Ancient

Chirand, on the northern bank of the Ganga River, in Saran district, has an archaeological record from the Neolithic age (about 2500–1345 BC). Regions of Bihar—such as Magadha, Mithila and Anga—are mentioned in religious texts and epics of ancient India.

Mithila gained prominence when people of Âryâvarta (an ancient name for India) established the Videha Kingdom. During the late Vedic period (c. 1100-500 BCE), Videha became one of the major political and cultural centers of South Asia, along with Kuru and Pañcâla. The kings of the Videha Kingdom were called Janakas. Sita, a daughter of one of the Janaks of Mithila is mentioned as the consort of Lord Rama, in the Hindu epic, Ramayana, written by Valmiki.

*Copy of the seal excavated from Kundpur, Vaishali. The Brahmi letters on the seal means: Kundpur was in Vaishali. Prince Vardhaman (Mahavira) used this seal after the Judgement*

The Videha Kingdom later became incorporated into the Vajjiconfederacy which had its capital in the city of Vaishali, which is also in Mithila. Vajji had a republican form of government where the king was elected from the number of rajas. Based on the information found in texts pertaining to Jainism and Buddhism, Vajji was established as a republic by the 6th century BCE, before the birth of Gautama Buddha in 563 BCE, making it the world's first republic.

The region of modern-day southwestern Bihar called Magadha remained the centre of power, learning, and culture in India for 1000 years. The Haryanka dynasty, founded in 684 BC, ruled Magadha from the city of Rajgriha (modern Rajgir). The two well-known kings from this dynasty were Bimbisara and his son Ajatashatru, who imprisoned his father to ascend the throne. Ajatashatru founded the city of Pataliputra which later became the capital of Magadha. He declared war and conquered the Vajji. The Haryanka dynasty was followed by the Shishunaga dynasty. Later the Nanda Dynasty ruled a vast tract stretching from Bengal to Punjab.

The Nanda dynasty was replaced by the Maurya Empire, India's first empire. The Maurya Empire and the religion of Buddhism arose in the region that now makes up modern Bihar. The Mauryan Empire, which originated from Magadha in 325 BC, was founded by Chandragupta Maurya, who was born in Magadha. It had its capital at Pataliputra (modern Patna). The Mauryan emperor, Ashoka, who was born in Pataliputra (Patna) is believed to be one of the greatest rulers in the history of the world.

The Gupta Empire, which originated in Magadha in 240 AD, is referred as the Golden Age of India in science, mathematics, astronomy, commerce, religion, and Indian philosophy. Bihar and Bengal was invaded by Rajendra Chola I of the Chola dynasty in the 11th century.

## Ancient History

The history of the land mass currently known as Bihar is very ancient. In fact, it extends to the very dawn of human civilization. Earliest myths and legends of Hinduism the Sanatana (Eternal) Dharma—are associated with Bihar. Sita, the consort of Lord Rama, was a princess of Bihar. She was the daughter of King Janak of Videha. The present districts of Muzaffarpur, Sitamarhi, Samastipur, Madhubani, and Darbhanga, in north-central Bihar, mark this ancient kingdom. The present small township of Sitamarhi is located here. According to legend, the birthplace of Sita is Punaura, located on the west-side of Sitamarhi, the headquarters of the district. Janakpur, the capital of King Janak, and the place where Lord Rama and Sita were married, lies just across the border in Nepal. It is reached via the rail station of Janakapur Road located in the Sitamarhi district, on the Narkatiyaganj—Darbhanga section of the North-Eastern Railway. It is no accident, therefore, that the original author of the Hindu epic—The Ramayana - Maharishi Valmiki - lived in Ancient Bihar.

Valmikinagar is a small town and a railroad station in the district of West Champaran, close to the railhead of Narkatiyaganj in northwest Bihar. The word Champaran is derived from champa-arnya, or a forest of the fragrant Champa (magnolia) tree.

It was here that Prince Gautam attained enlightenment, became the Buddha- at the present Bodh Gaya- a town in central Bihar; and the great religion of Buddhism was born. It is here also that Lord Mahavira, the founder of another great religion, Jainism, was born and attained nirvana (death). That site is located at the present town of pawapuri, some miles to the south east of Patna, the Capital of Bihar., it is here that the tenth and last Guru of the Sikhs, Guru Gobind Singh was born and attained the sainthood of Sikhism, that is became a Guru. A lovely and majestic Gurudwara (a temple for Sikhs) built to commemorate his memory—the harmandir— is located in eastern Patna. Known reverentially as the Patna Sahib, it is one of the five holiest places of worhip (Takhat) for Sikhs.

The ancient kingdoms of Magadha and of Licchavis, around about 7-8th century B.C., produced rulers who devised a system of administration that truly is progenitor of the modern art of statecraft, and of the linkage of statecraft with economics. Kautilya, the author of Arthashastra, the first treatise of the modern science of Economics, lived here. Also known as Chanakya, he was the wily and canny adviser to the Magadha king, Chandragupta Maurya. As an emissary of Chandragupta Maurya, Chanakya travelled far and wide in pursuit of promoting the interests of the State and dealing with the Greek invaders settled in the northwest of India, along the Indus valley. He succeded in preventing the further onslaught of the Greeks. Indeed, he brought about amicable coexistence between the Greeks and the Mauryan Empire. Megasthenes, an emissary of Alexander's General, Seleucus Necator, lived in Pataliputra (ancient name of Patna, the Mauryan capital) around 302 B.C.

He left behind a chronicle of life in and around Pataliputra. This is the first recorded account by a foreign traveller in India. It describes in vivid terms the grandeur of life in Pataliputra, a city established by King Ajatshatru, around 5th Century B.C., at the confluence of the rivers Sone and Ganga.

Another Mauryan king, Ashoka, (also known as Priyadarshi or Priyadassi), around 270 B.C., was the first to formulate firm tenets for the governance of a people. He had these tenets, the so called Edicts of Ashoka, inscribed on stone pillars which were planted across his kingdom. The pillar were crowned with the statue of one or more lions sitting on top of a pedestal which was inscribed with symbols of wheels. As the lion denoted strength, the wheel denoted the eternal (endless) nature of truth (dharma), hence the name Dharma (or Dhamma) Chakra.

This figure of lions, atop a pedestal, with inscription of a wheel, was adopted as the Official Seal of the independent Republic of India (1947). Also, Ashoka's dharma chakra was incorporated into the national flag of India, the Indian tricolour. Remains of a few of these pillars are still extant, for example at Lauriya-Nandan Garh in the district of West Champaran and at Vaishali, in the present district of the same name. Ashoka, a contemporary of Ptolemy and Euclid, was a great conqueror. His empire extended from what is now the North West Frontier Province (in Pakistan) in the west, to the eastern boundaries of present India in the north, and certainly, up to the Vindhyan Range in the south. Ashoka was responsible also for the widespread proselytization of people into Buddhism. He sent his son, Prince Mahendra, and daughter, Sanghamitra, for this purpose to as far south as the present country of Sri Lanka (Sinhal Dweep in ancient times, and Ceylon during the British Empire. Some historians, particularly Sinhalese, consider Mahindra and Sanghmitra as brother and sister.

Ancient Bihar also saw the glorification of women in matters of state affairs. It was here that Amrapali, a courtesan of Vaishali (the present district of the same name) in the kingdom of the Lichhavis, attained and wielded enormous power. It is said that the Lord Buddha, during his visit to Vaishali, refused the invitation of many princes, and chose to have dinner with Amrapali instead. Such was the status of women in the Bihari society of several centuries B.C.

A little-known, but historically and archaeologically documented, event is worth mentioning in this context. After his visit with Amrapali, Lord Buddha continued with his journey towards Kushinagar (also called Kusinara in Buddhist texts.) He travelled along the eastern banks of the river Gandak (also called Narayani, which marks the western border of Champaran, a district now administratively split into two- West and East Champaran.) A band of his devoted Licchavis accompanied Lord Buddha in this journey. At a spot known as Kesariya, in the present Purbi (meaning, East) Champaran district, Lord Buddha took rest for the night.

It was here that he chose to announce to his disciples the news of his impending niravana (meaning, death); and implored them to return to Vaishali. The wildly lamenting Licchavis would have none of that. They steadfastly refused to leave. Whereupon, Lord Buddha, by creating a 3,000 feet wide stream between them and himself compelled them to leave. As a souvenir he gave them his alms-bowl. The Licchavis, most reluctantly and expressing their sorrow wildly, took leave and built a stupa there to commemorate the event.

Lord Buddha had chosen that spot to announce his impending nirvana because, as he told his disciple Anand, he knew that in a previous life he had ruled from that place, namely, Kesariya, as a Chakravarti Raja, Raja Ben. (Again, this is not just a mere legend, myth or folklore. Rather, it is a historiclly documented fact supported by archaeological findings. However, neither this part of Buddha's life, nor the little town of Kesariya, is well-known even in India or Bihar.

At Nalanda, the world's first seat of higher learning, an university, was established during the Gupta period. It continued as a seat of learning till the middle ages, when the Muslim invaders burned it down. The ruins are a protected monument and a popular tourist spot. A museum and a learning centre- The Nava Nalanda Mahavira - are located here.

Nearby, Rajgir, was capital of the Mauryan Empire during the reign of Bimbisara. It was frequently visited by Lord Buddha and Lord Mahavira. There are many Buddhist ruins here. It is also well-known for its many hot-springs which, like similar hot-springs elsewhere in the world, are reputed to have medicinal property.

## Medieval

Buddhism in Magadha went into decline due to the invasion of Muhammad bin Bakhtiyar Khalji, during which many of the viharas and the famed universities of Nalanda and Vikramashila were destroyed. It was claimed that thousands of Buddhist monks were massacred during the 12th century. D. N. Jha suggests, instead, that these incidents were the result of Buddhist-Brahmin skirmishes in a fight for supremacy. In 1540, the great Pathan chieftain, Sher Shah Suri, from Sasaram, took northern India from the Mughals, defeating the Mughal army of Emperor Humayun. Sher Shah declared Delhi his capital.

From the 11th century to the 20th century, Mithila was ruled by various indigenous dynasties. The first of these where the Karnatas, followed by the Oinwar dynasty, Raghuvanshi and finally Raj Darbhanga. It was during this period that the capital of Mithila was shifted to Darbhanga.

The tenth and the last *Guru* of Sikhism, Guru Gobind Singh was born in Patna.

This glorious history of Bihar lasted till around the middle of the 7th or 8th century A.D. - the Gupta Period - when, with the conquest of almost all of northern India by invaders from the middle-east, the Gupta dynasty also fell a victim.

In medieval times Bihar lost its prestige as the political and cultural centre of India. The Mughal period was a period of unremarkable provincial administration from Delhi. The only remarkable person of these times in Bihar was Sher Shah, or Sher Khan Sur, an Afghan. Based at Sasaram which is now a town in the district of the same name in central-western Bihar, this jagirdar of the Mughal King Babur was successful in defeating Humayun, the son of Babur, twice - once at Chausa and then, again, at Kannauj (in the present state of Uttar Pradesh or U.P.) Through his conquest Sher Shah became the ruler of a territory that, again, extended all the way to the Punjab. He was noted as a ferocious warrior but also a noble administrator - in the tradition of Ashoka and the Gupta kings. Several acts of land reform are attributed to him. The remains of a grand mausoleum that he built for himself can be seen in today's Sasaram (Sher Shah's maqbara.)

## Colonial Era

After the Battle of Buxar (1764), the British East India Company obtained the diwani rights (rights to administer, and collect revenue or tax) for Bihar, Bengal and Odisha. The rich resources of fertile land, water and skilled labour had attracted the foreign imperialists, particularly the Dutch and British, in the 18th century. A number of agriculture-based industries had been started in Bihar by foreign entrepreneurs. Bihar remained a part of the Bengal Presidency of British India until 1912, when the province of Bihar and Orissa was carved out as a separate province. Since 2010, Bihar has celebrated its birthday as Bihar Diwas on 22 March.

## Pre- and post-Independence

Farmers in Champaran had revolted against indigo cultivation in 1914 (at Pipra) and 1916 (Turkaulia). In April 1917, Mahatma Gandhi visited Champaran, where Raj Kumar Shukla had drawn his attention to the exploitation of the peasants by European indigo planters. The Champaran Satyagraha that followed received support from many Bihari nationalists, such as Rajendra Prasad and Anugrah Narayan Sinha.

In the northern and central regions of Bihar, the Kisan Sabha (peasant movement) was an important consequence of the independence movement. It began in 1929 under the leadership of Swami Sahajanand Saraswati who formed the Bihar Provincial Kisan Sabha (BPKS), to mobilise peasant grievances against the zamindari attacks on their occupancy rights. The movement intensified and spread from Bihar across the rest of India, culminating in the formation of the All India Kisan Sabha (AIKS) at the Lucknow session of the Indian National Congress in April 1936, where Saraswati was elected as its first president.

Bihari migrant workers have faced violence and prejudice in many parts of India, such as Maharashtra, Punjab and Assam after independence.

## Modern History

During most of British India, Bihar was a part of the Presidency of Bengal, and was governed from Calcutta. As such, this was a territory very much dominated by the people of Bengal. All leading educational and medical centres were in Bengal. In spite of the unfair advantage that Bengalis possessed, some sons of Bihar rose to positions of prominence, by dint of their intelligence and hard labour. One such was Rajendra Prasad, native of Ziradei, in the district of Saran. He became the first President of the Republic of India.

When separated from the Bengal Presidency in 1912, Bihar and Orissa comprised a single province. Later, under the Government of India Act of 1935, the Division of Orissa became a separate province; and the Province of Bihar came into being as an administrative unit of British India. At Independence in 1947, the State of Bihar, with the same geographic boundary, formed a part of the Republic of India, until 1956. At that time, an area in the southeast, predominantly the district of Purulia, was separated and incorporated into West Bengal as part of the Linguistic Reorganization of Indian States.

Resurgence in the history of Bihar came during the struggle for India's independence. It was from Bihar that Mahatma Gandhi launched his civil-disobedience movement, which ultimately led to India's independence. At the persistent request of a farmer, Raj Kumar Shukla, from the district of Champaran, in 1917 Gandhiji took a train ride to Motihari, the district headquarters of Champaran. Here he learned, first hand, the sad plight of the indigo farmers suffering under the oppressive rule of the British.

Alarmed at the tumultuous reception Gandhiji received in Champaran, the British authorities served notice on him to leave the Province of Bihar. Gandhiji refused to comply, saying that as an Indian he was free to travel anywhere in his own country. For this act of defiance he was detained in the district jail at Motihari. From his jail cell, with the help of his friend from South Africa days, C. F. Andrews, Gandhiji managed to send letters to journalists and the Viceroy of India describing what he saw in Champaran, and made formal demands for the emancipation of these people.

When produced in court, the Magistrate ordered him released, but on payment of bail. Gandhiji refused to pay the bail. Instead, he indicated his preference to remain in jail under arrest. Alarmed at the huge response Gandhiji was receiving from the people of Champaran, and intimidated by the knowledge that Gandhiji had already managed to inform the Viceroy of the mistreatment of the farmers by the British plantation owners, the magistrate set him free, without payment of any bail.

This was the first instance of the success of civil-disobedience as a tool to win freedom. The British received, their first "object lesson" of the power of civil-disobedience. It also made the British authorities recognize, for the first time, Gandhiji as a national leader of some consequence. What Raj Kumar Shukla had started, and the massive response people of Champaran gave to Gandhiji, catapulted his reputation throughout India. Thus, in 1917, began a series of events in a remote corner of Bihar, that ultimately led to the freedom of India in 1947.

Sir Richard Attenborough's award winning film, "Gandhi", authentically, and at some length, depicts the above episode. (Raj Kumar Shukla is not mentioned by his name in the film, however.) The two images here are from that film. The bearded gentleman, just behind Gandhiji, in the picture on the left, and on the elephant at right, is Raj Kumar Shukla.

Gandhiji, in his usual joking way, had commented that in Champaran he "found elephants just as common as bullock carts in (his native) Gujarat"

It was natural, therefore, that many people from Bihar became leading participants in India's struggle for independence. Dr. Rajendra Prasad has been mentioned above. Another was Jay Prakash Narayan, affectionately called JP. JP's substantial contribution to modern Indian history continued up until his death in 1979.

It was he who steadfastly and staunchly opposed the autocratic rule of Indira Gandhi and her younger son, Sanjay Gandhi. Fearing people's reaction to his opposition, Indira Gandhi had him arrested on the eve of declaring National Emergency beginning June 26, 1975. He was put in the Tihar Jail, located near Delhi, where notorious criminals are jailed.

Thus, in Free India, this septuagenerian, who had fought for India's freedom alongside Indira Gandhi's father, Jawahar Lal Nehru, received a treatment that was worse than what the British had meted out to Gandhiji in Champaran in 1917, for his speaking out against oppression. The movement started by JP, however, brought the Emergency to an end, led to the massive defeat of Indira Gandhi and her Congress Party at the polls, and, to the installation of a non-Congress government - The Janata Party—at Delhi, for the first time. With the blessings of JP, Morarji Desai became the fourth Prime Minister of India. JP remained the Conscience of the Janata Party and of post-Gandhi—post-Nehru India. He gave a call to all Indians to work ceaselessly towards eliminating "dictatorship in favour of democracy" and bringing about "freedom from slavery". Sadly, soon after attaining power, bickerings began among the leaders of the Janata Party which led to the resignation of Shri Desai as the Prime Minister. JP continued with his call for "total revolution" (sampporna kranti), but he succumbed to kidney failure at a hospital in Bombay in 1979.

Subsequent bickerings in the Janata Party led to the formation of a breakaway political party - the Janata Dal. This political party is a constituent unit of the current ruling coalition at Delhi, the so called, United Front. It was also from this party that Laloo Prasad Yadav, the Chief Minister of Bihar was elected. The bickering continued. A new party led by Mr. Yadav was formed as—the Rashtriya Janata Dal- which went on to rule for almost 15 years in Bihar.

This was also a period when Hindi literature came to flourish in the state. Raja Radhika Raman Singh, Shiva Pujan Sahay, Divakar Prasad Vidyarthy, Ramdhari Singh Dinkar, Ram Briksha Benipuri, are some of the luminaries who contributed to the flowering of Hindi literature, which did not have much of a long history.

The Hindi language, certainly its literature, began around mid to late nineteenth century. It is marked by the appearance of Bhartendu Babu Harischandra's (a resident of Varanasi in U.P.) drama "Harischandra". Devaki Nandan Khatri began writing his mystery novels in Hindi during this time (Chandrakanta, Chandrakanta Santati, Kajar ki Kothari, Bhootnath, etc.) He was born at Muzaffarpur in Bihar and had his earlier education there. He then moved to Tekari Estate in Gaya in Bihar. He later became an employee of the Raja of Benares (now Varanasi.) He started a printing press called "Lahari" which began the publication of a Hindi monthly, "Sudarshan", in 1898. One of the first short stories in Hindi, if not the very first, was "Indumati" (Pundit Kishorilal Goswami, author) which was published in 1900. The collection of short stories "Rajani aur Taare" (Anupam Prakashan, Patna, publishers) contains an extended history of the origin and evolution of the short story as a distinct literary form in the Hindi literature.

## Timelines

- 560-480 BCE: Buddha
- Before 325 BCE: Nanda clan in Magadha, Licchavis in Vaishali
- 325-185 BCE: Maurya Dynasty

- 250 BCE: 3rd Buddhist Council
- 185 BCE-80 CE: Sunga Dynasty
- 80 - 240: Regional kings
- 240 - 600: Gupta Dynasty
- 600 - 650: Harsha Vardhana
- 750 - 1200: Pala Dynasty
- 1200: Muhammad of Ghori's army, destroys the universities at Nalanda and Vikramshila
- 1200-1250: Decline of Buddhism
- 1250-1526: Ruled by Delhi Sultanate (Muslim Turks—Tughluqs, Sayyids, Lodis)
- 1526-1540: Babur defeats last Delhi sultan, establishes Mughal Empire
- 1540-1555: Suri dynasty captures empire from Mughals (including Shershah Suri who built the Grand Trunk Road)
- 1526-1757: Mughal dynasty resumes
- 1757-1857: British East India Company rule
- 1857: Revolt of 1857
- 1857-1947: British Raj rule
- 1912: Province of Bihar & Orissa separated from Bengal
- 1935: Bihar and Orissa become separate provinces
- 1947: Indian Independence; Bihar becomes a state
- 2000: Bihar divided into two states - north part remains "Bihar", southern becomes Jharkhand

"Bihar" has been derived from the word "Vihar" which was symbol of Buddhist monasteries. Bihar is one of the places which has seen the birth of ancient civilisation and Indian history. Hindu, Buddhist, Jain, Muslim and Sikh Shrines abound in this ancient land where India's first major empire rose and fell. It is land of not only the religious preachers but also of Emperors and great warriors. It had four Kingdoms: Mithila (Videh), Vaishali Ang and Magadha.

***Videh:*** During Vedic days Videh was ruled by Janak vanshi kings and Raja Janak ,"Sita's" father who was one of the kings. During 6th century B.C. this place had the first elected republic of the world. During the course of time, eight small republics were formed which later on merged with Lichhavi State.

***Vaishali:*** Vishal the son of Surya Vansha formed the Vaishali state. During 6th century B.C. Vaishali became a republic state.

***Ang:*** This state was established by a prince named Angad. Full details of this state is not available in the history except that Ang king married his daughter to Kaushambi king Udayan to save his kingdom from Puruthan the king of Magadha. Still this Kingdom could not be saved as Bimbisar of Haryak vansh conquered Ang and merged it with Magadha.

***Magadha:*** The area of Patna and Gaya constituted the ancient Magadha kingdom having it's capital at Rajgrih. Barahyadrath, father of Jarasandh established the Magadha kingdom in 6th century B.C. Later on Bimbisara became the ruler of Magadha. Bimbisara and Ajatshatru expanded their Kingdom covering northern Bihar. Thereafter Shishunag became the ruler and conquered Awauti state.

During 4th century B.C. Ugrasen of Nand Vansh became the ruler, who was dethroned by Chanakya and his disciple Chandragupta. Chandragupta was a great warrior who forced Sikander to leave India and also conquered Afghanistan & Baluchistan and made it a part of his kingdom. Chandragupta was succeeded by Bindusar and then by Ashoka the Great, who ruled from 273 century BC to 232 BC. King Ashoka became the follower of Buddhist religion after he attacked Kaling in which 1 million people were killed and 1.5 million people were taken as prisoners.

He spread Buddhism throughout the world. History of next 500 years are not of great importance. From 26th Feb 320 AD rule of Gupta regime started and Chandragupta first became the king. He made Pataliputra his kingdom and ruled till 330 AD. His son Samudragupta ruled from 330 AD to 380 AD.

And degeated 12 kings of south and became famous throughout the world. Samudragupta's son Chandragupta Vikramadutt became the ruler from 375 AD to 493 AD and conquered Gujrat, Kathivada & Ujjaini. The great poet Kalidas was one of the Ratna's of that period. Maukhri Vansh ruled Bihar for some time followed by Harshvardhan, Sashank & Adityasen.

During 743 AD Palvansh ruled Magadha and the ruler were Gopal, Dharampal and Deopal. After the death of Deopal the kingdom started disintegrating. During 1236, Muslims attacked Bihar but Shershah Suri (1472-1545) brought stability again. Akbar, the great made Bihar a separate state consisting Magadha, Tirhut and Ang . Suja became the Governor of Bihar. In 1652 the British started business form Patna and after Palasi war they started ruling Bihar . The British ruled Bihar from 1765 to 1947 and thereafter Bihar became a state under the Union of India.

## PUBLIC HEALTH

In Bihar, attempts have been made to establish a well-functioning department of public health. National efforts like the National Health Mission, the Clinical Establishments Act of 2010, and the formation of the Empowered Action Group (EAG) catalyze the disbursement of federal funds by expanding healthcare access and improving the quality of healthcare services to states in need. However, Bihar's ability to fully utilize this funding is lacking. Bihar's health care system has the appropriate policies in place to allow for the implementation of comprehensive healthcare treatment. However, it is in the execution and management of the funding and services where it falls behind. Overall, the lack of consistent monitoring tools for policy evaluation explain why a strategic, evidence based public health system has been slow to take root in the state of Bihar. Consequently, Bihar generally ranks weakest in health outcomes in comparison to other Indian states and even among its EAG counterparts.

Research indicates that Bihar relies on privatized hospitals to provide healthcare to the masses, it has high levels of unacknowledged corruption and also implements a vertical system of disease management. In fact, the ratio of private spending on health care relative to public spending in Bihar is the second highest in India. These factors have been found to be associated with slower healthcare delivery and a higher degree of economic burden as a consequence of steep healthcare costs. Much of this is because Bihar lacks in the continuity and transparency of health reporting as required by the Clinical Establishments Act of 2010. In turn, this prevents the government from making evidence based conclusions about policy changes and hospital effectiveness. Rather, Bihar's health department displays patterns of ill-informed spending, inconsistent hiring, and erratic spending on healthcare infrastructure.

For example, according to the Government of India's "Ministry of Health & Family Welfare Health and Family Welfare Census Data 2008-2015", the number of healthcare professionals including registered nurses, auxiliary nurses, physicians and health supervisors at each hospital in Bihar have remained significantly lower compared to those working in Kerala, and do not seem to follow any sort of pattern. Rather, its number of registered healthcare professionals remains constant over time. Compared to Bihar, we see that Kerala's number of registered healthcare professionals consistently increase over time. According to "Rural Health Statistics 2015", the greatest shortfalls exist among physicians and specialists across the state at least 75%. This extends to the number of actual health centers across Bihar as well, as it only has 50% of the sub health centers, 60% of the primary health centers, and a mere 9% of the community health centers it needs based on the national government's supply to population norms. At a closer look, the number of hospital beds that Bihar includes in each government run hospital actually decreased between 2008 and 2015, compared to the consistently increasing number of hospital beds in government run Kerala hospitals. Given the population of Bihar (population: 99 million) is much denser than Kerala (population: 35 million), these numbers suggest that Bihar is significantly behind in the number of healthcare professionals that should be employed within the state. It is likely that because there is a lack of data reporting, analysis and evaluation within Bihar that these trends exist.

Despite these shortcomings, Bihar has shown gradual signs of public health improvement in a few areas. There is indeed a shortage of skilled healthcare professionals, but Bihar still benefits from a surplus of female health workers compared to male health workers. In terms of key impact indicators, between 2010 and 2013, the crude birth rate decreased by 2.3%, crude death rate decreased by 5.6%, infant mortality rate decreased by 12.7%, neo-natal mortality rate decreased by 8.6%, under 5 mortality rate decreased by 9.1%, and maternal mortality ratio decreased by 10.2%.

It would suit Bihar well to continue to adapt common cost effective practices to strengthen their health systems data measurement and research. Research has shown that the implementation of patient and caregiver surveys, exit interviews at health centers, vignettes, and audit studies are simple methods of bolstering reporting and evaluation in lower income areas such as Bihar.

## MEDIA

*Biharbandhu* was the first Hindi newspaper published in Bihar. It was started in 1872 by Madan Mohan Bhatta, a Marathi Brahman who settled in Bihar Sharif. Hindi journalism in Bihar, and specially Patna, could make little headway initially. Many Hindi journals were born and, after a lapse of time, vanished. Many journals were shelved even in the planning stages. But once Hindi had the support of being an official language, it started making inroads, even into the remote areas of Bihar. Hindi journalism acquired wisdom and maturity, and its longevity was assured. Hindi was introduced in the law courts in Bihar in 1880.

Urdu journalism and poetry has a glorious past in Bihar. Many poets belong to Bihar, such as Shaad Azimabadi, Kaif Azimabadi, and Kalim Ajiz. Shanurahman, a world-famous radio announcer, is from Bihar. Many Urdu dailies— such as *Qomi Tanzim* and *Sahara*—are published in Bihar. There is a monthly Urdu magazine called *Voice of Bihar* – which is the first of its kind and is becoming popular among the Urdu speaking people.

The beginning of the 20th century was marked by a number of notable new publications. A monthly magazine named *Bharat Ratna* was started in Patna, in 1901. It was followed by *Ksahtriya Hitaishi*, *Aryavarta from Dinapure*, *Udyoga*, and *Chaitanya Chandrika*. *Udyog* was edited by Vijyaanand Tripathy, a famous poet of the time, and *Chaitanya Chandrika*by Krishna Chaitanya Goswami, a literary figure of that time. The literary activity was not confined to Patna alone but to other districts of Bihar.

*Hindustan*, *Dainik Jagran*, *Rajasthan Patrika*, *Aaj*, and *Prabhat Khabar* are some of the Hindi newspapers of Bihar. National English dailies like *The Times of India*, *Hindustan Times*, *Navbharat Times*, *The Telegraph*, and *The Economic Times* have readers in the urban regions.

# 2

# Culture and Society

## CULTURE

### Paintings

There are several traditional styles of painting practiced in Bihar. One is Mithila painting, a style of Indian painting used in the Mithila region of Bihar.Traditionally, painting was one of the skills that was passed down from generation to generation in the families of the Mithila region, mainly by women. Painting was usually done on walls during festivals, religious events, and other milestones of the life cycle, like birth, Upanayanam (the sacred thread ceremony), and marriage.

Mithila painting was traditionally done on huts' freshly plastered mud walls, but today it is also done on cloth, handmade paper, and canvas. Famous Mithila painters have included Smt Bharti Dayal, Mahasundari Devi, the late Ganga Devi, and Sita Devi.

Mithila painting is also called Madhubani art. It mostly depicts human beings and their association with nature. Common scenes illustrate deities like Krishna, Ram, Shiva, Durga, Lakshmi, and Saraswati from ancient epics. Natural objects like the sun, moon, and religious plants like tulsi are also widely painted, along with scenes from the royal court and social events like weddings. Generally no space is left empty.

Historically, the Patna School of Painting (*Patna Salaam*), sometimes called *Company Painting*, flourished in Bihar during the early 18th to mid-20th centuries.

The Patna School of Painting was an offshoot of the well-known Mughal Miniature School of Painting. Those who practiced this art form were descendants of Hindu artisans of Mughal painting.

Facing persecution from the Mughal Emperor, Aurangzeb, these artisans found refuge, via Murshidabad, in Patna during the late 18th century. Their art shared the characteristics of the Mughal painters, but whereas the Mughal style depicted only royalty and court scenes, the Patna artists also started painting bazaar scenes.

They used watercolours on paper and on mica. The style's subject matter evolved to include scenes of Indian daily life, local rulers, festivals, and ceremonies. This school of painting formed the basis for the formation of the Patna Art School under the leadership of Shri Radha Mohan. The School is an important center of fine arts in Bihar.

## Performing arts

*Vidyapati*

*Magahi folk singers*

*Bharat Ratna Ustad Bismillah Khan, from Dumraon, Bihar*

Bihar has produced musicians like Bharat Ratna Ustad Bismillah Khan and dhrupad singers like the Malliks (Darbhanga Gharana) and the Mishras (Bettiah Gharana) along with poets like Vidyapati Thakur who contributed to Maithili Music. The classical music in Bihar is a form of the Hindustani classical music. Gaya is another centre of excellence in classical music, particularly of the Tappa and Thumri varieties. PanditGovardhan Mishra – son of the Ram Prasad Mishra, himself an accomplished singer – is perhaps the finest living exponent of Tappa singing in India today, according to Padma Shri Gajendra Narayan Singh, founding secretary of the Sangeet Natak Academi of Bihar. Gajendra Narayan Singh also writes, in his memoir, that Champanagar, Banaili, was another major centre of classical music. Rajkumar Shyamanand Sinha of Champanagar, Banaili princely state, was a great patron of music and was himself one of the finest exponents of classical vocal music in Bihar in his time. Singh, in another book on Indian classical music, has written that "Kumar Shyamanand Singh of Banaili estate had such expertise in singing that many great singers including Kesarbai Kerkar acknowledged his ability. After listening to bandishes from Kumar Sahib, Pandit Jasraj was moved to tears and lamented that, alas!, he did not have such ability himself." [free translation of Hindi text].

During the 19th century, when the condition of Bihar worsened under the British misrule, many Biharis had to emigrate as indentured labourers to the West Indies, Fiji, and Mauritius. During this time many sad plays and songs called *birha* became popular, in the Bhojpur region, thus *Bhojpuri Birha*. Dramas incorporating this theme continue to be popular in the theatres of Patna.

## Cinema

Bihar has a robust Bhojpuri-language film industry. There is also a smaller production of Magadhi-, Maithili-, as well as Angika-language films. The first film with Bhojpuri dialogue was *Ganga Jamuna*, released in 1961. Bhaiyaa, the first Magadhi film, was released in 1961. The first Maithili movie was *Kanyadan* released in 1965. Maithili film Mithila Makhaan won the National Film Award for Best Maithili Film in 2016. The history of films entirely in Bhojpuri begins in 1962 with the well-received film *Ganga Maiyya Tohe Piyari Chadhaibo* ("Mother Ganges, I will offer you a yellow sari"), which was directed by Kundan Kumar. 1963's *Lagi nahin chute ram* was the all-time hit Bhojpuri film, and had higher attendance than Mughal-e-Azam in the eastern and northern regions of India. Bollywood's *Nadiya Ke Paar* is another of the most famous Bhojpuri-language movies. However, in the following years, films were produced only in fits and starts. Films such as *Bidesiya* ("Foreigner", 1963, directed by S. N. Tripathi) and *Ganga* ("Ganges", 1965, directed by Kundan Kumar) were profitable and popular, but in general Bhojpuri films were not commonly produced in the 1960s and 1970s.

In the 1980s, enough Bhojpuri films were produced to tentatively support a dedicated industry. Films such as *Mai* ("Mom", 1989, directed by Rajkumar Sharma) and *Hamar Bhauji* ("My Brother's Wife", 1983, directed by Kalpataru) continued to have at least sporadic success at the box office. However, this trend faded out by the end of the decade, and by 1990, the nascent industry seemed to be completely finished.

The Bhojpuri film industry took off again in 2001 with the super hit *Saiyyan Hamar* ("My Sweetheart", directed by Mohan Prasad), which vaulted the hero of that film, Ravi Kishan, to superstardom. This success was quickly followed by several other remarkably successful films, including *Panditji Batai Na Biyah Kab Hoi* ("Priest, tell me when I will marry", 2005, directed by Mohan Prasad) and *Sasura Bada Paisa Wala* ("My father-in-law, the rich guy", 2005). In a measure of the Bhojpuri film industry's rise, both of these did much better business in the states of Uttar Pradesh and Bihar than mainstream Bollywood hits at the time, and both films, made on extremely tight budgets, earned back more than ten times their production costs. *Sasura Bada Paisa Wala* also introduced Manoj Tiwari, formerly a well-loved folk singer, to the wider audiences of Bhojpuri cinema. The success of Ravi Kishan & Manoj Tiwari's films has led to a dramatic increase in Bhojpuri cinema's visibility, and the industry now supports an awards show and a trade magazine, *Bhojpuri City*, which chronicles the production and release of what are now over one hundred films per year.

## BIHARI CULTURE

Bihari culture refers to the culture of the Indian state of Bihar. Bihari culture includes Mithila culture, Bhojpuri Culture and the culture of Magadha.

### Language and literature

Hindi is the official languages of the State. Maithili and Urdu are other recognised languages of the state. Unrecognised languages of the state are Bhojpuri, Angika and Magahi. Bhojpuri and Magahi are sociolinguistically a part of the Hindi

Belt languages fold, thus they were not granted official status in the state.The number of speakers of the Bihari languages is difficult to count because of unreliable sources. In the urban region, most educated speakers of the language name Hindi as their language because this is what they use in formal contexts and believe it to be the appropriate response because of unawareness. The uneducated and the rural population of the region regards Hindi as the generic name for their language.

Despite of the large number of speakers of Bihari languages, they have not been constitutionally recognized in India, except Maithili which is recognised under the Eighth Schedule of the Constitution of India. Hindi is the language used for educational and official matters in Bihar. These languages was legally absorbed under the subordinate label of Hindi in the 1961 Census. Such state and national politics are creating conditions for language endangerment. The first success for spreading Hindi occurred in Bihar in 1881, when Hindi displaced Urdu as the sole official language of the province. In this struggle between competing Hindi and Urdu, the potential claims of the three large mother tongues in the region – Bhojpuri, Maithili and Magahi were ignored. After independence Hindi was again given the sole official status through the Bihar Official Language Act, 1950. Urdu became the second official language in the undivided State of Bihar on 16 August 1989. Bihar also produced several eminent Urdu writers including Sulaiman Nadvi, Manazir Ahsan Gilani, Abdul Qavi Desnavi, Paigham Afaqui, Jabir Husain, Sohail Azimabadi, Hussain Ul Haque, Dr. Shamim Hashimi, Wahab Ashrafi etc.

Bihar has produced a number of writers of Hindi, including Raja Radhika Raman Singh, Shiva Pujan Sahay, Divakar Prasad Vidyarthy, Ramdhari Singh 'Dinkar', Ram Briksh Benipuri, Phanishwar Nath 'Renu', Gopal Singh "Nepali" and Baba Nagarjun. Mahapandit Rahul Sankrityayan, the great writer and Buddhist scholar, was born in U.P. but spent his life in the land of Lord Buddha, i.e., Bihar. Hrishikesh Sulabh and Neeraj Singh (from Ara) are the prominent writer of the new generation. They are short story writer, playwright and theatre critic. Arun Kamal and Aalok Dhanwa are the well-known poets. Different regional languages also have produced some prominent poets and authors. Sharat Chandra Chattopadhyay, who is among the greatest writers in Bengali, resided for some time in Bihar. Upamanyu Chatterjee also hails from Patna in Bihar. Devaki Nandan Khatri, who rose to fame at the beginning of the 20th century on account of his novels such as *Chandrakanta* and *Chandrakanta Santati*, was born in Muzaffarpur, Bihar. Vidyapati Thakur is the most renowned poet of Maithili (c. 14–15th century). Satyapal Chandra has written many English bestseller novels and he is one of India's emerging young writer.

Bihar has also produced some prominent poets and authors who write in various regional languages:

- Sharat Chandra Chattopadhyay, who is among the most prominent authors who writes in Bengali, resided for some time in Bihar.
- The latest Indian author who writes in English, Upamanyu Chatterjee, also hails from Patna in Bihar.
- Devaki Nandan Khatri, who rose to fame at the beginning of the 20th century with his novels *Chandrakanta* and *Chandrakanta Santati*, was born in Muzaffarpur, Bihar.
- Vidyapati Thakur, who wrote around the 14th to 15th centuries, is the most renowned Maithili-language poet In India.
- Satyapal Chandra has written many critically acclaimed best-sellers in English.

## Drama and theatre

In 1984, Satish Anand had evolved a new 'Bidesia Style' for modern Indian theatre. The new style used elements of traditional folk theatre from indigenous Bihari culture. Some other traditional Bihari forms of theatre include those centred around Raja Salhesh, and the festival of Sama Chakeva originating from the Mithila region of Bihar.

## Sculpture

The first sculptures in Bihar date back to the Mauryan Empire. The Pillars of Ashoka and Didarganj Yakshi are estimated to be at least 2000 years old, and were carved out of a single piece of stone. Ancient statues are found throughout Bihar.

Some of these sculptures were made from bronze, an advanced technique at that time. For example, the Sultanganj Buddha statue, estimated to be 1500 years old, is about seven feet tall and made of 500 kg of bronze, making it the largest statue of that period. Many statues, ranging from Hellenistic gods to various Gandharan lay devotees, are combined with what are thought to be early representations of the Buddha and Bodhisattvas.

Today, it is still unclear exactly when the Greco-Buddhist art of Gandhara emerged. However, evidence from Sirkap indicates that this style of art was already highly developed before the advent of the Kushans. Mandar Hill features the unique image of Lord Vishnu, from the Gupta period, in his man-lion incarnation. The image is 34 inches high and made of black stone.

Most of the Hindu and Buddhist sculptures in Bihar were destroyed by Muslim invaders, as in the other major centers of Hinduism and Buddhism in India.

## Cuisine

The Bihari staple food is a dish composed of roti, dal, chawal, sabzi, and achar. It is prepared from lentils, wheat flour, rice, vegetables, and pickle. The traditional cooking medium is mustard oil. Customarily, Biharis eat a boiled rice-based lunch and roti-based dinner and breakfast. Khichdi, a broth of rice and lentils seasoned with spices and served with several accompanying items, constitutes the mid-day meal for most Hindu Biharis on Saturdays. The favourite dish among Biharis is litti-chokha. Litti is made up of sattu, while chokha is made of smashed potatoes, tomatoes and brinjals.

Bihar offers a large variety of sweet delicacies which, unlike those from Bengal, are mostly dry. These include Chena Murki, Kala Jamun, Kesaria Peda, Khaja, Khurma, Pua & Mal Pua, Thekua, Murabba and Tilkut. Many of these originate in towns in the vicinity of Patna. Other salted snacks and savouries popular in Bihar include Litti, Makhana and Sattu.

Historically, the foods of eastern Uttar Pradesh and western Bihar were strongly influenced by Mughalai cuisine. This resulted in the development of Bhojpuri cuisine with Bihari flavor, reflecting Bihar's unique confluence of cultures.

***Regional specialties***

Some of the regions within Bihar have traditionally developed their own specialty dishes. For example, Anga is known for Chitba (a flour and sugar pancake) and Pitthow (a rice-based dish), as well as Tilba and Chewda of Katarni rice. Kadhi bari is another popular favorite which consists of fried soft dumplings made of besan (gram flour) that are cooked in a spicy gravy of yogurt. This dish is often eaten with plain rice.

In Mithilanchal, the food culture has traditionally been both vegetarian and non-vegetarian. Cuisine from the region tends to be similar to Bengali cuisine, although it tends to use mustard oil and the five spices known as the "Paanch Phoron." Popular dishes include Machchak Jhor, a special fish curry made in a spicy mustard paste; Kankorak Chokha, a mashed preparation of roasted crab; Ramruch, a besan-based dish; and Dokak Jhor, an oyster stew cooked with onion gravy. Another traditional dish from this region is Maus, which is generally mutton, chicken, or squails (tittar/battair) in a spicy gravy, usually eaten with malpuas. A traditional sweet dish called Bagiya which are dumplings made up of rice flour and stuffed with khoya is also popular in rural areas

## Religion

In Bihar, every aspect of life is suffused with religious significance and its manifestations abound in every corner of the state. Shrines are numerous, and religious symbols or images of deities abound. Many Biharis keep religious symbols, statues, and the like in their homes, vehicles, and offices. A typical Bihari household begins each day with religious devotion.

Most religious festivals in the region stem from Hinduism, given that it is the state's predominant religion. There are many variations on the festival theme. While some are celebrated all over the state, others are observed only in certain areas. In one region or another, festivals take place round the year. Many festival days are officially proclaimed as government holidays.

## MUSIC OF BIHAR

Bihar is a state of India. The classical form of the Indian music is already quite well known and the classical music in Bihar is but a form of the Hindustani classical music. Hence this article deals with the folk culture of Bihar which is rather distinctive.

Bihar is among the few Indian states which has a rich subaltern culture. The region's folk songs are associated with the various events in the life of an ordinary person. There are songs like sohar - performed during childbirth, sumangali - associated with wedding, ropnigeet - performed during the season of sowing paddy, katnigeet - performed during the paddy harvesting season, purbi, chaita, hori, bidesia, ghato, birha, kajari, irni/ birni, pachra, jhumar, jatsari, aalah, nirgun, and samdaun. There is also the tradition of war songs called Beer Kunwar.

The influence of Bihari music in seen in regions such as Mauritius, South Africa and the Caribbean, where a large of Bihari indentured labourers were taken as coolies during the nineteenth century.

There is a great tradition of folk songs started by Bhikhari Thakur, the redoubtable artist from the Bhojpur region.

Other wandering folk singers include the Kathaks, who travelled in groups and performed accompanied by dholak, sarangi, tamburu and majira. Other musician classes included Roshan Chouki, Bhajaniya, Kirtaniya, Pamaria and Bhakliya.

## HISTORY OF CLASSICAL MUSIC

Based on the research and findings of Shri Alakh Narain Prasad of Patna. Shri Prasad was a well-known musician in Patna as well as Bihar and was known for patronizing musicians from all over the country. The annual event of Ganesh Puja at his place was well known through out Bihar where renowned musicians used to gather for 2-3 evenings and also included other items like one-act play, skits, etc.

There was a time when interested people used to find out places where music of various kinds was arranged. They used to attend such places where musical programs were arranged.

In the forties, musicians of high caliber were appointed and trained by the help of rajahs, maharajahs, nawaabs and zamindars in various states (provinces) and estates of India. Bihar was no less than any other state in patronizing the classical music and its exponents with full sympathy and hospitality which was a culture embedded in the people of Bihar and Patna was not an exception.

There were small estates in Bihar, Patna having a few. These estates had their own musicians individually and a kind of competitions used to be organized to select the best musicians who performed during some special occasions and festivals.

Musicians considered Patna as one of the main seats of Music in the country and they used to come and perform here. Particularly during the festival of Durga Puja, they never neglected Patna and used to come and perform on the stage specially built for the occasion. Such stages were built at many places in Patna and programs were chalked out. People, all night long, used to see the performances of the artists and enjoyed the music.

Several local artists of Patna and they also participated. Music was in the air everywhere for three-four days during the Dussehara in Patna and the outside musicians were so much entertained that they didn't miss an opportunity to praise the hospitality of the Patnaites. Some of them were so impressed that they did not want to leave Patna and were tempted to settle down permanently.

In North Bihar, there was the Darbhanga estate , where several musicians were appointed for the Durbar both instrumentalists and vocalists. One of the vocalists, Pandit Ram Chatur Mullick was well versed in Dhrupad, Dhammaar and Thumri styles of classical music. He was also an outstanding musician of All India Radio, Patna.

During those times, the musicians of durbars were not allowed to go out to perform nor were they allowed to earn money by going to several doors unless they were permitted on request by other parties for the performance with the condition that they will not charge any money. They were warned thus because they were given all the remuneration from the durbar and this was done only to save the prestige of the musicians and the durbar itself.

There was another estate of Bettiah. This estate also had musicians and Pandit Deepraj among them was an expert in Dhrupad. He was so popular and favorite due to his musical talents that the "raaj" had bestowed upon him plots of land ('jagirs') for the maintenance of his whole family and the coming generations.

The landlord (zamindaar) of Pachhgachhia, Rai Bahadur Lakshminarain Singh was himself a learned person in classical music and was an exponent in playing the "pakhawaj" (a percussion instrument). He trained many musicians in "Shashtriya Sangeet" (Classical Music). One of his best disciple was Magan Khawas who had earned quite a reputation even outside Bihar. Unfortunately, he died very young at the age of 35.

Another student of the Rai Bahadur was Raghu Jha who was also a very expert musician. He was an artist of the All India Radio, Patna.

Then there was Ghana Ram, a great musician of the durbar of Maharaja of Dumraon. He had composed Ragas in quite a different and peculiar styles which have now become rare and most of them lost in the flow of time. Those who are aware of them, are still interested to know them. It makes a good research subject.

The rajahs of the Banaily estate were also very fond of music and they had appointed musicians (gaayeks) of high caliber in their durbar. The entire family of the rajahs had knowledge of music. One Ustaad Iltaaf Hussain Khan, who was an outstanding musician of the All India Radio, Patna, lived in Baneily with Raja Saheb. He had participated several times in the National Program of All India Radio, Delhi which was a matter of great prestigious status.

A big zamindaar (landlord) of Muzaffarpur, Uma Shankarji, alias Bacha Babu, was well versed in the Dhrupad style of classical music. He also had several musicians in his durbar and Ustad Kalay Khan and his brother Ustad Najju Khan were his famous durbar musicians. Both brothers were known for excelling in Raga Dhrupad. Najju Khan was also an exponent of Khayal, Thumri and Ghazals.

Bacha Babu gave due respects to the artists of other states by inviting them at his place. Artists like Sangeet Martand Pandit Vinayak Rao Patvardhan, Pundit Onkarnath and many other renowned musicians were regularly invited at his place. Ram Hari Dandekar, a musician and a disciple of Pundit Vinayak Rao Patvardhan, was in his durbar for providing training in classical music to the children of Bacha Babu.

At Arrah, there was another zamindaar of Jamira estate, Shatrunjay Prasad Singh alias Lallan Babu, who was a great lover of classical music. He left no stone unturned in preserving the sanctity of classical music by holding annual music conferences. He himself was a master in playing the Pakhawaj and the Tabla and trained several students whom to play these two percussion instruments.

In Gaya, there was Maharaj Deo who was also fond of classical music and used to invite famous musicians belonging to other states during the festivals of Holi and Dussehara. People of Gaya had always been music lover and in Pawai, which was then a village, several musicians lived. (Gaya people are very fond of music and still keeping the tradition for introducing music of high class).

Some of the musicians remained in Patna for good seeing the interest, involvement and appreciation for music. Ustaad Aman Khan of Rampur in Uttar Pradesh, remained in Patna till his last breath. He was exponent in the Dhrupad and Dhammaar styles of classical music.

A very renowned singer named Bari Zohra Bai lived in Patna for a very long period. She was an expert singer in the styles of 'Khayaal" and "Thumri". Her songs were recorded by the renowned recording company "His Master's Voice" (or more popularly known as HMV) and her records were very hot during those days. She was much appreciated and patronized by the Ramgarh Estate of Bihar and the Maharaja of Gidhaur had given her handsome rewards.

There was one Mushtary Bai of Agra exponent in the "Khayaal", "Thumri" and "Tappa" style of music and she also stayed in Patna for years.

Then there was Baurahi Kaneez, who was expert in singing the "Thumri", "Daadraa" and "Kajli" styles of Indian Classical Music. She also spent her life in Patna.

As for instrumental music, it is to be noted that Harmonium, which was an essential instrument for accompaniment with the musicians, was introduced in Bihar by Pandit Ganpat Rao (alias Bhaiyaji) who was an eminent Veenkaria of Gwalior in Madhya Pradesh. He lived in Patna for years and made some famous disciples like Sohni ji of Gaya and Patna's Ustaad Ghafoor Khan who were very famous for playing harmonium. Bhaiya Ji used to live in Patna with one Pandit Keshav Maharaj who himself was an exponent player of "Pakhawaj" and "Tabla", the famous percussion instruments. Keshav Maharaj was the pioneer of spreading music among the amateurs in Patna. His famous disciple was Pundit Shyam Narain Singh who played the harmonium. He was also the Music Teacher in the famous Girls' High School of Patna.

As regards 'Tabla', another important percussion instrument, Ustaad Ali Qadar Khan was quite famous. His son Daddan Khan was just like his father as far as Tabla playing was concerned. His fame spread due to being an expert in "Taal Kaharwa", a type of rhythm which is somehow more popular than other types of rhythms.

"Sarangi" has also been a very important string instrument for accompaniment with the singers. Among the old Sarangi players, Shiva Sahay Ji, Shambhu Guru, Hira Guru and Mukut Guru were famous. They were wizards in giving a faithful combinations of "swaras" (musical notes) while accompanying with famous vocalists. Bahadur Khan was also a famous Sarangi player and was equally expert in harmonium. Bahadur Khan's son Ata Hussain Khan was a good vocalist who was also an eminent artist of the All India Radio, Patna. He also always remained in Patna.

Some other vocalists were also residents of Patna. Ustaad Sadique Khan (who was also an expert in playing the Sitaar); Gul Mohammed Khan, expert in Khayaal in the Kirana Gharana ( a family tradition) style; Roshan Ara, daughter of Patna based Chanda Bai, learned music in Patna but later settled in Bombay (now Mumbai) where she got appreciation and kept the prestige of Patna. She was nicknamed Maua. Then, there were other singers of repute like Haider, Imam Bandi and Ramdasi. Ramdasi was a very promising musician in the Khayaal style and Bhajans trained by Mukut Guru but she died very young. These famous classical music exponents were the jewels of Patna.

Patna also had good Kathak Nritya dancers. (Kathak is one of the classical styles of dance of North India). There was one Thapa Guru who was a famous Kathak dancer. At that time there was a group of Bhaands (dancers) whose leader was Alijaan. In every festival, specially in marriages, it had become a prestigious custom to arrange for the dances of the Bhaands and without Alijaan and his party the Mehfil (the function) was considered to be incomplete. Alijaan was an accomplished vocalist too and was expert in rendering the Thumri style of classical music. While singing, his expressions and poses were excellent and well enjoyed by the audience.

Speaking of Thumri, we can mention the name of Karim Khan Saheb of Gwalior. He was a high class Thumri Gayak (singer). The "boles" (wordings) of Thumri were his originality. He was always invited to Patna during the festivals for his performances. Dussehara was the main festival when the renowned and reputed musicians were invited to Patna. Due to the various musical programs, Patna's Dussehara was famous in the whole country. Musical functions were organized at different Chaurahas (cross roads) under the banners of various Puja Committees. For two, and sometimes three days every year during the festival, day and night, music dominated the atmosphere. The people of Patna, males, females, children, old and young, all used to enjoy the music these two or three days by moving from chauraha to chauraha. They wanted to hear all the good artists and so they moved the whole night and enjoyed music.

Some famous artists who came to Patna every year were Pandit Onkaar Nath; Pandit Vinayak Rao Patwardhan; Faiyaaz Khan Saheb; Aaftaab-e Maushiqui, Pandit Narayan Rao Vyas; Pandit Manhar Barway; Pundit D. V. Paluskar (son of the famous Pundit Vishnu Digambar Paluskar; Ram Marathe(the famous actor and director of Indian cinema); Ustaad Ali Akbar Khan (the great Sarod, a string instrument, player); Ustaad Mushtaaq Ali Khan (Sitar player); Hira Bai Barodkar, Saraswati Rane; and, great Kathak Dancer and Sangeet Samraat Sukrey Maharaj with his party consisting of his daughter Sitara Bai and son Gopikrishna, brother-in-law Chaturbhuj Chaubey. These artists were from places like Calcutta, Mumbai, Poona, Gwalior, Nepal etc. Apart from them, of course, the artists of Bihar, as named earlier, participated.

Patna has always been in the forefront for keeping up the tradition of classical, light classical and light music and has always given the opportunity to all the musicians not only of

Bihar but of the country by providing them with the appropriate platform for their performance and appreciating their innate talents. Patna has always been adorned with music and musicians and the people, even today, are keeping up the tradition. For the last many many years, Patna has been the centre and seat of music. Today of course, there has been a change in the sense that classical music has been overshadowed by the modern trend of music such as the Pop, film music and other very light music. This is due to changes on the social, political, cultural and educational fronts. However, Patna always encouraged the classical musicians who were attracted towards Patna and used to come and perform in the presence of rich as well as the poor and the middle class people and all of them enjoyed their music. Patna always paid them great respect and provided proper hospitality.

## MUSIC COLLEGES BIHAR

In Bihar, music is quite a favorite subject among the people and many who get a chance try to learn it.

In order to help you explore the various music colleges in Bihar and the colleges that provide BA in music, we have, on this page, tried to list all the institutes and colleges that provide music courses in Bihar. This list of music institutes in India has been compiled from various sources. We have tried our best to provide accurate and updated details about the music colleges in Bihar providing various music courses including BA in Music. However, if you encounter any discrepancy in the BA music colleges or the music institutes provided here, do write to us. We welcome any kind of feedback that will improve the quality of the site, a site that strives to provide the best information regarding music institutes and courses in Bihar.

# 3

# Government and Politics

## GOVERNMENT AND ADMINISTRATION

The constitutional head of the government of Bihar is the governor, who is appointed by the President of India. The real executive power rests with the chief minister and the cabinet. The political party or the coalition of political parties having a majority in the Legislative Assembly forms the government.

The head of the bureaucracy of the state is the chief secretary. Under this position, is a hierarchy of officials drawn from the Indian Administrative Service, Indian Police Service, Indian Forest Service, and different wings of the state civil services. The judiciary is headed by the Chief Justice. Bihar has a High Court which has been functioning since 1916. All the branches of the government are located in the state capital, Patna.

The state is divided into nine divisions and 38 districts, for administrative purposes. Bihar has 12 Municipal Corporations, 49 Nagar Parishads, and 80 Nagar Panchayats.

### Politics

By 2004, 14 years after Lalu Prasad Yadav's victory, *The Economist* magazine said that "Bihar [had] become a byword for the worst of India, of widespread and inescapable poverty, of corrupt politicians indistinguishable from mafia-dons they patronise, caste-ridden social order that has retained the worst feudal cruelties". In 2005, the World Bank believed that issues faced by the state were "enormous" because of "persistent poverty, complex social stratification, unsatisfactory infrastructure and weak governance". Currently, there are two main political formations: the National Democratic Alliance (NDA) which comprises Bharatiya Janata Party, Lok Janashakti Party, Rashtriya Lok Samta Party, Hindustani Awam Morcha and JD(U) (Joined recently after breaking the Grand Alliance with RJD and INC), Second is alliance between RJD and Indian National Congress. There are many other political formations. The Communist Party of India had a strong presence in Bihar at one time, but is weakened now. The CPM and Forward Bloc have a minor presence, along with the other extreme Left.

*Vidhansabha Building, Patna*

In contrast to prior governments, which emphasised divisions of caste and religion, Nitish Kumar's manifesto was based on economic development, curbs on crime and corruption and greater social equality for all sections of society. Since 2010, the government has confiscated the properties of corrupt officials and redeployed them as schools buildings. Simultaneously they introduced Bihar Special Court Act to curb crime. It has also legislated for a two-hour break on Fridays, including lunch, to enable Muslim employees to pray and thus cut down on post-lunch absenteeism by them. The government has prohibited the sale and consumption of alcohol in the state since March 2016; this ban has been linked to a drop in tourism to Bihar.

## GOVERNMENT OF BIHAR

The Government of Bihar, known locally as the State Government, is the supreme governing authority of the Indian state of Bihar and its 9 divisions which consist of 38 districts . It consists of an executive, led by the Governor of Bihar, a judiciary and legislative branches.

Like other states in India, the head of state of Bihar is the Governor, appointed by the President of India on the advice of the central government. His or her post is largely ceremonial. The Chief Minister is the head of government and is vested with most of the executive powers. Patna is the capital of Bihar.

The Patna High Court, located in Patna, has jurisdiction over the whole state.

The present legislative structure of Bihar is bicameral.The Legislative houses are the Bihar Vidhan Sabha (Bihar Legislative Assembly) and Bihar Vidhan Parishad (Bihar Legislative Council). Their normal term is five years, unless dissolved earlier.

### First Government

1946:First Cabinet of Bihar formed; consisting of two members,Dr. Sri Krishna Sinha as first Chief Minister of Bihar and Dr. Anugrah Narayan Sinha as Bihar's first Deputy Chief Minister cum Finance Minister (also in charge of Labour,Health,Agriculture and Irrigation).Other ministers were inducted later.The Cabinet served as the first Bihar Government after independence in 1947.

## ADMINISTRATION IN BIHAR

Bihar is a state situated in North India. It is surrounded by West Bengal to the east, Uttar Pradesh to the west, Jharkhand to the south and Nepal to the north.

### *History*

Before 1905, Bihar was a part of British East India Company's Bengal Presidency. In 1905 the Bengal Presidency was divided and created two new provinces: East Bengal and West Bengal. Until then Bihar was part of West Bengal. Again West Bengal and East Bengal reunited in 1911 but the people of Bihar and Orrisa demanded a separate province based on language rather than religion. In 1912 Bihar and Orissa Province was created separating from Bengal Presidency. In 1936, Bihar and Orrisa Province divided into two new provinces: Bihar Province and Orissa Province.

### *Bihar and Orissa Province*

Following Divisions were included in Bihar and Orissa Province when it separated from Bengal Presidency in 1912:

- Bhagalpur Division (districts of Bhagalpur, Munger (Monghyr), Purnea and the Sonthal Parganas)
- Patna Division (Gaya, Patna and Shahabad)
- Tirhut Division (Champaran, Darbhanga, Muaffarpur and Saran)
- Chota Nagpur Division (Hazaribagh, Manbhum, Palamau, Ranchi and Singhbhum)
- Orissa Division (Angul, Balasore, Cuttack, Puri and Sambatpur)

On 1 April 1936 Bihar and Orissa Province was divided into two new provinces: Bihar Province and Orissa Province

### *Bihar Province*

In 1936, Bihar became a separate province including part of Jharkhand.

After the independence of India in 1951, Bihar including Jharkhand had 18 districts, and had 55 districts in 1991.

### *Bihar*

In 2000, Bihar again divided into two states: the current Bihar and Jharkhand. In 2001 Bihar had a total of 37 districts.

## Administrative structure

Structurally Bihar is divided into divisions (Pramandal), districts (jila), blocks (Prakhand), municipal corporations (Nagar Nigam), municipalities(Nagar Parishad) and city councils (Nagar Panchayat).

The state is divided into 9 divisions, 38 districts, 534 blocks, 12 municipal corporations, 49 Nagar Parishads and 80 Nagar Panchayats, for administrative purposes. The various districts included in the divisions—Patna, Tirhut, Saran, Darbhanga, Kosi, Purnia, Bhagalpur, Munger and Magadh Division.

# JUDICIARY

## High Court

The Patna High Court is the High Court of the state of Bihar. It was established on February 3, 1916, and later affiliated under the *Government of IndiaAct, 1915*. The court is headquartered in Patna, the administrative capital of the state.

A proclamation was made by the Governor-General of India on 22 March 1912. The foundation-stone of the High Court Building was laid on 1 December 1913 by His Excellency the late Viceroy and Governor-General of India, Sir Charles Hardinge of Penshurst. The Patna High Court building on its completion was formally opened by the same Viceroy on 3 February 1916. Hon. Sir Justice Edward Maynard Des Champs Chamier was the first Chief Justice of Patna High Court.

This High Court has given two Chief Justices of India: Hon'ble Mr. Justice Bhuvaneshwar Prasad Sinha, the 6th C.J.I., and Hon. Mr. Justice Lalit Mohan Sharma, the 24th C.J.I..

Hon. The Chief Justice Mr. Rajendra Menon is the current Chief Justice of Patna High Court. He assumed his office on 15 March 2017.

## Legislature

Bihar is one of the seven states where bicameral legislature exists. Other states are Uttar Pradesh, Karnataka, Maharashtra, Jammu and Kashmir, Telangana and Andhra Pradesh. The Vidhan Parishad serves as the upper house and Vidhan Sabha serves as the lower house of a bicameral legislature.

### *Vidhan Sabha*

The Vidhan Sabha is also known as Legislative Assembly. The Bihar Legislative Assembly first came into being in 1937. The current strength of the House is 243.

### *Vidhan Parishad*

The Vidhan Parishad is also known as Legislative Council.

A new province of Bihar and Orissa was created by the British Government on 12 December 1911. The Legislative Council with a total of 43 members belonging to different categories was formed in 1912. The first sitting of the Council was convened on 20 January 1913. In 1936, Bihar attained its separate Statehood. Under the Government of India Act, 1919, the unicameral legislature got converted into bicameral one, i.e. the Bihar Legislative Council and the Bihar Legislative Assembly. Under the Government of India Act, 1935, the Bihar Legislative Council consisted of 29 members. After the first General Elections 1952, the number of members was increased up to 72 and by 1958 the number was raised to 96. With the creation of Jharkhand, as a result of the Bihar Reorganisation Act, 2000 passed by the Parliament, the strength of the Bihar Legislative Council has been reduced from 96 to 75 members.

## POLITICS OF BIHAR

The Politics of Bihar, a state in eastern India, was characterised, in the early 2000s, by weak governance and corrupt politicians.Currently, there are four main political Parties: Rashtriya Janata Dal, Janata Dal (United), Bharatiya Janata Party and Lok Janshakti Party.

All four along with some smaller regional parties like Rashtriya Lok Samata Party and Hindustani Awam Morcha are playing vital role in bihar politics. while Indian National Congress is a small player in Bihar Politics. Bihar is currently ruled by Janta Dal (United) and Bhartiya Janta Party coalition.

## Administration and Governments

The constitutional head of the Government of Bihar is the Governor, who is appointed by the President of India. The real executive power rests with the Chief Minister and the cabinet. The political party or the coalition of political parties having a majority in the Legislative Assembly forms the Government.The first Chief Minister of Bihar was Sri Krishna Sinha & first Deputy Chief Minister was Dr Anugrah Narayan Sinha.

Previous Chief Minister Jitan Ram Manjhi, succeeded Nitish Kumar, who resigned after Lok Sabha Polls (General Elections) in 2014 taking responsibility of JDU's deplorable performance. Again Nitish Kumar became the Chief Minister of Bihar after Jitan Ram Manjhi was sacked.

The head of the bureaucracy of the State is called the Chief Secretary. Under him is a hierarchy of officials drawn from the Indian Administrative Service, Indian Police Service, and different wings of the State civil services. The judiciary is headed by the Chief Justice. Bihar has a High Court which has been functioning since 1916. All the branches of the government are located in the state capital, Patna.

The state is divided into 9 divisions and 38 districts, for administrative purposes. The various districts included in the divisions – Patna, Tirhut, Saran, Darbhanga, Kosi, Purnia, Bhagalpur, Munger and Magadh Division, are as listed below.

## History

### *Pre-Independence*

Bihar was an important part of India's struggle for independence. Gandhi became the mass leader only after the Champaran Satyagraha that he launched on the repeated request of a local leader, Raj Kumar Shukla, he was supported by great illumanaries like Dr. Rajendra Prasad, Dr. Anugrah Narayan Sinha and Brajkishore Prasad.

### *Post Independence : 1950–1975*

The first Bihar governments in 1946 were led by two eminent leaders Sri Babu (Dr. Sri Krishna Sinha) and Anugrah Babu (Dr. Anugrah Narayan Sinha) who were men of unimpeachable integrity and great public spirit.They ran an exemplary government in Bihar.

After Independence of India, the power was shared by these two great Gandhiannationalists Dr. Sri Krishna Sinha who later became the first Chief Minister of Bihar and Dr. Anugrah Narayan Sinha who decidedly was next to him in the cabinet and served as the first Deputy Chief Minister cum Finance Minister of Bihar.

Bihar was rated as the best administered among the states in the country at that time.In late 60's death of central railway minister late Mr. Lalit Narayan Mishra (who was killed by a hand grenade attack for which central leadership is blamed most of the time) pronounced the end of indigenous work oriented mass leaders. For two decades congress ruled the state with the help of puppet chief ministries hand in glove with the central government (Mrs. Indira Gandhi) ignoring the welfare of the people of the state. It was the time when a prominent leader like Satyendra Narayan Singh took sides with the Janata Party and deserted congress from where his political roots originated, following the ideological differences with the congress.

### *Bihar movement & Aftermath: 1975–1990*

After independence also, when India was falling into an autocratic rule during the regime of Indira Gandhi, the main thrust to the movement to hold elections came from Bihar under the leadership of Jayaprakash Narayan. In 1974, JP led the student's movement in the state of Bihar which gradually developed into a popular people's movement known as the Bihar Movement. It was during this movement that Narayan gave a call for peaceful Total Revolution together with V. M. Tarkunde, he founded the Citizens for Democracy in 1974 and the People's Union for Civil Liberties in 1976, both NGOs, to uphold and defend civil liberties.On 23 January 1977, Indira Gandhi called fresh elections for March and released all political prisoners. Emergency officially ended on 23 March 1977.The Congress Party, suffered a defeat at the hands of the Janata Party coalition of several small parties created in 1977 and the alliance came to power, headed by Morarji Desai, who became the first non-Congress Prime Minister of India. In Bihar, the Janata Party won all the fifty-four Lok Sabha seats in 1977 general elections under the mentorship of Narayan and rose to power in Bihar assembly also. Karpoori Thakur became Chief Minister after winning a contest from the then Janata Party President Satyendra Narayan Sinha.

Bihar movement's campaign warned Indians that the elections might be their last chance to choose between "democracy and dictatorship."

This resulted in two things:

- The identity of Bihar (from the word Vihar meaning monasteries) representing a glorious past was lost. Its voice often used to get lost in the din of regional clamour of other states, specially the linguistic states like Uttar Pradesh, Madhya Pradesh etc.
- Bihar gained an anti-establishment image. The establishment-oriented press often projected the state as indiscipline and anarchy.

Idealism did assert itself in the politics from time to time, viz, 1977 when a wave defeated the entrenched Congress Party and then again in 1989 when Janata Dal came to power on an anti corruption wave. In between, the socialist movement tried to break the stranglehold of the status quoits under the leadership of Mahamaya Prasad Sinha and Karpoori Thakur. This could not flourish, partly due to the impractical idealism of these leaders and partly due to the machinations of the central leaders of the Congress Party who felt threatened by a large politically aware state. Communist Party in Bihar was formed in 1939. In the 1960s, 1970s and 1980s the Communist movement in Bihar was a formidable force and represented the most enlightened section in Bihar. The movement was led by veteran communist leaders like Jagannath Sarkar, Sunil Mukherjee, Rahul Sankrityayan, Pandit Karyanand Sharma, Indradeep Sinha, and Chandrashekhar Singh. It was under the leadership of Sarkar that the Communist party fought "total revolution" led by Jayprakash Narayan, as the movement in its core was anti-democratic and challenged the very fabric of Indian democracy.

Since the regional identity was slowly getting sidelined, its place was taken up by caste-based politics, power initially being in the hands of the Brahmins, Bhumihars and Rajputs.

### *Lalu's Politics : 1990–2004*

Janata Dal came to power in the state in 1990 on the back of its victory at the national stage in 1989. Lalu Prasad Yadav became Chief Minister after winning the race of legislative party leadership by a slender margin against Ram Sundar Das, a former chief minister from the Janata Party and close to eminent Janata Party leaders like Chandrashekhar and S N Sinha. Later, Lalu Prasad Yadav gained popularity with the masses through a series of popular and populist measures. The principled socialists, Nitish Kumar included, gradually left him and Lalu Prasad Yadav was the uncrowned king by 1995 as both Chief Minister as well as the President of his party, Rashtriya Janata Dal. He was a charismatic leader who had people's support and Bihar had got such a person as the chief minister after a long time. But he couldn't bring the derailed wagon of development of the state on to the track. When corruption charges got serious, he quit the post of CM but anointed his wife as the CM and ruled through proxy. In this period, the administration deteriorated fast.

### *After 2004*

2008 (Politics): By 2004, 14 years after Lalu's victory, The Economist magazine said that "Bihar [had] become a byword for the worst of India, of widespread and inescapable poverty, of corrupt politicians indistinguishable from mafia-dons they patronise, caste-ridden social order that has retained the worst feudal cruelties". In 2005, the World Bank believed that issues faced by the state was "enormous" because of "persistent poverty, complex social stratification, unsatisfactory infrastructure and weak governance".

In 2005, as disaffection reached a crescendo among the masses, middle classes included, the RJD was voted out of power and Lalu Prasad Yadav lost an election to a coalition headed by his previous ally and now rival Nitish Kumar. Nitish Kumar has regained Bihar's true identity, which is the place from where people who changed the world come like Gautam Buddha or Asoka or Sher Shah Suri or the Sikh Gurus. Despite the separation of financially richer Jharkhand, Bihar has actually seen more positive growth in recent years.

Currently, there are three main political formations: Janata Dal, Bharatiya Janata Party and the Rashtriya Janata Dal led coalition which also has the Indian National Congress. There are myriad other political formations. Ram Vilas Paswan led Lok Janshakti Party is a constituent of the NDA at the centre, and does not see eye to eye with Lalu Prasad Yadav's RJD in Bihar. Bihar People's Party is a small political formation in north Bihar. The Communist Party of India had a strong presence in Bihar at one time, but has got weakened now. CPM and Forward Bloc have minor presence. Ultra left parties like

CPML, Party Unity etc. have presence in pockets and are at war with the state.

## ELECTIONS IN BIHAR

Elections in Bihar state, India are conducted in accordance with the Constitution of India. The Assembly of Bihar creates laws regarding the conduct of local body elections unilaterally while any changes by the state legislature to the conduct of state level elections need to be approved by the Parliament of India. In addition, the state legislature may be dismissed by the Parliament according to Article 356 of the Indian Constitution and President's rule may be imposed.

## Bihar electoral system

### *National level representation*

Lok Sabha delegation : The Indian general election, 2009 in Bihar were held for 40 seats with the state going to polls in the first four phases of the general elections. The major contenders in the state were the National Democratic Alliance (NDA), Indian National Congress and the Fourth Front. NDA consisted of the Bharatiya Janata Party (BJP) and Janata Dal (United) whereas the fourth front was constituted of the Rashtriya Janata Dal (RJD), Lok Jan Shakti Party (LJP) and the Samajwadi Party (SP).

### *Rajya Sabha delegation*

Both the houses of the state legislature jointly nominate Members of Parliament to the Rajya Sabha.The Rajya Sabha or Council of States is the upper house of the Parliament of India. Membership of Rajya Sabha is limited by the Constitution to a maximum of 250 members, and current laws have provision for 245 members. Most of the members of the House are indirectly elected by state and territorial legislatures using single transferable votes, while the President of India can appoint 12 members for their contributions to art, literature, science, and social services. Members sit for staggered six-year terms, with one third of the members retiring every two years.

## State level representation

### *Legislative assembly*

Bihar legislature assembly has 243 seats. For the election of its members, the state is divided into 243 Assembly Constituencies in which the candidate securing the largest number of votes is declared elected. In the Bihar Assembly Elections, 2010, the National Democratic Alliance formed the state government having secured a simple majority of 206 seats.Bihar Legislative Assembly came into existence in 1937. The Assembly had a strength of 152 members. According to the provisions of the Constitution of India, the first General Elections in the state were held in 1952. The total strength of membership in the Assembly was 331, including one nominated member. Dr Sri Krishna Singh became the first Leader of the house and the Chief Minister and Dr Anurag Narayan Sinha was elected the first deputy leader of the assembly and became state's first Deputy Chief Minister. It was reduced to 318 during the second General Elections. In 1977, the total number of elected members of the Bihar Legislative Assembly was further raised from 318 to 324. With the creation of a separate State of Jharkhand, by an Act of Parliament titled the Bihar Reorganisation Act, 2000, the strength of the Bihar Legislative Assembly was reduced from 325 to 243 members. The current Nitish Kumar government is a minority, powered by the Congress, RJD and CPI to majority status

### *Legislative Council*

The upper house known as the Legislative Council has lesser powers than the Assembly and several of its members are nominated by the Assembly. Others are elected from various sections of the society like Graduates and Teachers. Currently the Legislative Council consists of 95 members. A new Province of Bihar and Orissa was created by the British Government on 12 December 1911. The Legislative Council with a total of 43 members belonging to different categories was formed in 1912. The first sitting of the Council was convened on 20 January

1913. In 1936, Bihar attained its separate Statehood. Under the Government of India Act, 1919, the unicameral legislature got converted into bicameral one, i.e. the Bihar Legislative Council and the Bihar Legislative Assembly.

Under the Government of India Act, 1935, the Bihar Legislative Council consisted of 29 members. After the first General Elections 1952, the number of members was increased up to 72 and by 1958 the number was raised to 96. With the creation of Jharkhand, as a result of the Bihar Reorganisation Act, 2000 passed by the Parliament, the strength of the Bihar Legislative Council has been reduced from 96 to 75 members.

## POLITICS

Bihar was at the forefront of India's struggle of independence. Right from the 1857 war of independence to the 1942 Quit India movement, the whole country looked to Bihar for providing direction to its freedom struggle. Gandhi became the mass leader only after the Champaran Satyagraha that he launched on the repeated request of a local leader, Rajkumar Shukla. After independence also, when India was falling into an autocratic rule during the regime of Indira Gandhi, the main thrust to the movement to reinstate democracy came from Bihar under the leadership of Jaya Prakash Narayan.

This has resulted in two things:

1. There is no regional identity for the state. Its voice often gets lost in the din of regional clammer of other states, specially the linguistic states like Tamil Nadu, Gujarat, Andhra etc.
2. Bihar has gained an anti establishment image. The establishment oriented press often projects this as indiscipline and anarchy.

Since the regional identity did not develop, its place was taken up by caste based politics, power initially being in the hands of the Brahmins and Bhumihars. Idealism did assert itself in the politics from time to time, viz, 1977 when a wave defeated the entrenched Congress Party and then again in 1989 when Janta Dal came to power on an anti corruption wave.

In between, the socialist movement tried to break the stanglehold of the status quoists under the leadership of Mahamaya Prasad Sinha and Karpoori Thakur. Unfortunately, this could not flourish, partly due to the impractical idealism of these leaders and partly due to the machinations of the central leaders of the Congress Party who felt threatened by a large politically aware state.

Janata Dal came to power in the state in 1990 on the back of its victory at the national stage in 1989. Laloo Prasad Yadav became Chief Minister after winning the race of legialative party leadership by a slender margin against Ramsundar Das, a low caste politician with an enviable record of public service.

Later, Laloo gained popularity with the masses through a series of popular and populist measures. The principled socialists, Nitish Kumar included, gradually left him and Laloo was the uncrowned king by 1995 as both Chief Minister as well as the President of his party, Rashtriya Janata Dal. When corruption charges got serious, he quit the post of CM but anointed his wife as the CM and ruled through proxy. In this period, the administration deteriorated fast.

In 2005, as disaffection reached a crescendo among the masses, middle classes included, the RJD was voted out of power and Laloo Prasad lost an election to a coalition headed by his previous ally and now rival Nitish Kumar.

Currentlly, there are two main political formations: the NDA which comprises of Janata Dal and Bharatiya Janata Party and the Rashtriya Janata Dal led coalition which also has the Indian National Congress.

There are myriad other political formations. Ram Vilas Paswan led Lok Janshakti Party is a constituent of the UPA at the centre, but does not see eye to eye with Laloo Prasad Yadav's RJD in Bihar. Bihar People's Party is a small political formation in north Bihar. The Communist Party of India had a strong presence in Bihar at one time, but has got weakened now. CPM and Forward Bloc have minor presence. Ultra left parties like CPML, Party Unity etc have presence in pockets and are at war wtih the state.

## MOVEMENT FOR SEPARATION

The movement for separation of Bihar from Bengal was the first effort to assert her own regional identity in terms of sub-nationalism. At the regional level, participation for separate Bihar 'facilitated through the aggregation of primordial loyalities like religious group, caste association and the regional identities' 85.

The westernised Bihari elites were carriers of this movement. Three major factors, namely Bihari intelligentsia, Bengali settlers and British imperialism interacted and determined the character of the regional and economic consciousness of Bihar.

Let us first discuss the factor of indigenous elites 'The historians have tried to characterize this class as an elite group and have sought to emphasise the determining role of the attitude and social behaviour of this group to the exclusion of more basic structural feature of the economy'.

The movement for separate Bihar was spearheaded by the professional and the educated elites and not by the Bihari entrepreneurs. This is because of preponderance of feudalism in Bihar.

The social bases of these elites were limited. The movement in Bihar mainly revolved round the discrimination against Biharis in the matter of education and jobs. The movement had no wider ramification.

Being essentially movement for separation of Bihar, it could not build bridges with the boycott movement of Bengal (1905). Non-participation in 'Swadeshi' movement seriously effected the intellectual outlook of the movement in the sphere of developing independent economic agenda. Ironically, during the 'Swadeshi' movement, when more than three hundred units were functioning in Orissa, in contrast only three committees were functioning in Bihar. Even these committees were mainly functional in Bhagalpur. As they were mainly manned by Bengali settlers, they were contemptuously referred as 'Babu Tamasha'.

The class limitation of the movement for separation of Bihar is reflected by the absence of any political thought based on economic nationalism. Without contesting the justification of the demand for reservation of jobs for the local people, they could not transcend the movement beyond it. The British imperialism further distorted economic and social development of Bihar. While Industrial Revolution was sweeping in England, Gangetic belt in India, specially in Bihar was experiencing systematic process of deindustrialization which was staggering.

Now let us take up the second factor, namely, the Bengali settlers. Despite the political linkage of Bihar with Bengal, linguistically and culturally she was more connected with Hindi Heartland.

This lack of cultural affinity restrained the Bengali settlers to identify with local population. In addition, the former developed supercilious attitude of cultural superiority as a result of their dominance as subordinate partner in the administrative professional set-up in the colonial rule.

Except some noteworthy but limited contributions, they could not emerge as the main conveyor belt for the dispersal of the radical ideas that emerged in Bengal earlier along with the social and political awakening.

This is rather natural because these people were part of the colonial administration; 'a middle class' of Bengal could not play the historical role in initiating cultural renaissance in backward area.

One of the weaknesses of Bengali renaissance was its geographical limitations, with no significant spill over to Bihar. Some reformist movement like Brahma Samaj, though implanted in Bihar, could not develop root in the soil. It is a dismal failure of the so called Bengali renaissance to establish powerful link with Bihar and thereby breaking its conservative insularity. This lack of activities on the part of Bengal with transregional perspective particularly in the backward peripheries, also determined the character of the superstructural complexion of Bihar. Secondly, because of its elitist character, Bengal remained more or less indifferent to the general problems of Bihar.

For example, Bengal successfully fought against the monstrous oppression of indigo planters in the 19th century; but she did not extend this movement to Bihar. Infact, Bihar had to wait nearly half a century for Gandhi to organise crusade against the indigo planters.

In this movement, Bihar was caught in the whirlwind of nationalism of Gandhian era without sufficiently developing sub-nationalism. So, Bihar developed nationalism in which regional identity was stuck up in the quagmire of caste and to a certain extent in the sub-regional entities like Maithili, Jharkhand, Bhojpuri etc.

The third factor, as mentioned earlier, is the colonial rule. The boycott movement of Bengal induced the imperialist rulers to take steps so that no militant movement similar to Bengal, might develop in Bihar. The British Government was facing organized resistance in Bengal. With the partition of Bengal, 'Swadeshi' movement was organised successfully there. The middle class Bengali youth were organizing 'revolutionary activities'. The situation compelled the British Government to show their support to the voices of protest raised in Bihar against the employment of Bengalis.

Subsequently, Bihar became the most important bastion of national movement during the Gandhian era. This shift towards all India political linkage of Bihar is extremely significant. First, it denotes the most significant reality of Indian politics in the emergence of the western India on the national movement.

The geographical connotation actually indicates the increasing domination of industrial capitalist from western India over other parts of India including Bihar and also in the Indian National Congress along with the group of different regional elites, who earlier assumed its leadership.

The Congress party became 'loose confederation of interests' which 'could integrate in the colonial period the multiple levels of nationalism in India'89. The earlier reluctance of the Sethias in Bombay to be drawn to even in the initial stage of anti-British political trend, faded away to a certain extent.

Their contradictions with imperialism made them realize the importance of the platform of Indian National Congress which could be transformed into a powerful instrument to foster their class interest. On the other hand, the middle class elites needed the support of a powerful financial class to sustain the tempo of the national movement.

## BHARATIYA JAN CONGRESS

Bharatiya Jan Congress (Indian Popular Congress) was a political party that existed in the Indian state of Bihar around 1999-2001. BJC was led by the ex-Chief Minister Jagannath Mishra.

Mishra, who then belonged to the Indian National Congress, was the Chief Minister of Bihar 1975-1979, 1980-1983 and 1989-1990. Mishra was an opponent of the leadership of Sitaram Kesri in the Congress party.

Mishra was accused for corruption in connection with the so-called 'fodder scandal'. During one period he has imprisoned for his role in the affair.

In 1999 BJC was active in forming a political front in Bihar consisting of BJC, Bihar Vikas Party, Janata Dal (Secular), All India Forward Bloc, Samajwadi Janata Party and Nationalist Congress Party. The front was supposed to confront both the National Democratic Alliance and Rashtriya Janata Dal. The BJC youth wing was called Bharatiya Yuva Jan Congress (Indian Youth Popular Congress) and the student wing Bharatiya Chhatra Jan Congress (Indian Student Popular Congress). In 2001 BJC merged with Nationalist Congress Party. Mishra did however leave NCP ahead of the 2004 elections and joined Janata Dal (United).

## BIHAR PEOPLE'S PARTY

Bihar People's Party was a political party in the Indian state of Bihar, founded by Rajput strongman and former leader of the Samajwadi Krantikari Sena paramilitary faction Anand Mohan Singh. Singh had previously been a member of Janata Dal, Samata Party and All India Rashtriya Janata Party. He had been elected to Lok Sabha as a SAP candidate in 1996 and as a AIRJP candidate in 1998. The wife of Singh, Lovely Anand, was a high-profile leader of BPP. BPP merged with the Indian National Congress on February 28 2004.

## BIHAR VIKAS PARTY

Bihar Vikas Party (Bihar Development Party), political party in the Indian state of Bihar. BVP was formed ahead om the Lok Sabha 1999 by BJP Rajya Sabha MP, Janardan Yadav. Yadav got some local ex-BJP leaders along to his new party. Yadav got 6 591 votes (1,04%) in the constituency Godda (today part of Jharkhand). BVP are opponents of the bifurcation of Bihar and the creation of Jharkhand as a separate state. BVP stands on the same ideological ground as BJP, for example on the Ayodhya issue.

## KISAN VIKAS PARTY

Kisan Vikas Party (Peasant Development Party), a small political party in the Indian state of Bihar. It is probably a splinter-group from the BJP.

## KRANTIKARI SAMYAVADI PARTY

Krantikari Samyavadi Party (Revolutionary Communist Party) is an Indian political party in the state of Bihar.

KSP was formed as a splinter-group from Communist Party of India. KSP wanted to continue cooperation with Laloo Prasad Yadav's Rashtriya Janata Dal. In the state assembly elections 2000 KSP won two seats (supported by Laloo). In total the party had put up seven candidates. The relation with RJD was later broken. In the Lok Sabha elections 2004 KSP had launched a candidate in Madhubani, who got 6 948 votes (1% of the votes in that constituency).

## RASHTRAWADI KISAN SANGHATAN

Rashtrawadi Kisan Sanghatan (Nationalist Farmers Organization), a political party founded by the landlord paramilitary group Ranvir Sena, in Bihar, India. RKS was formed by the Sena in order to make it possible for it to contest elections.

## RASHTRIYA JANATA DAL (DEMOCRATIC)

Rashtriya Janata Dal (Democratic) (National People's Party (Democratic)), political party in India, formed when a group of five MPs (three Lok Sabha, two Rajya Sabha) broke away from Rashtriya Janata Dal 2001. RJD(D) joined National Democratic Alliance and RJD(D) leader Nagmani became a minister in the government of Vajpayee 2003. Later the same year RJD(D) merged with BJP.

## SAMAJWADI KRANTIKARI SENA

The Samajwadi Krantikari Sena (Socialist Revolutionary Army) is a political front and militia group in the Indian state of Bihar founded in 1980 by Anand Mohan Singh (a Rajput strongman). The group fought against different groups belonging to lower castes. The prime objective of the Sena was to work against reservation quotas for lower castes. Mohan later joined the Janata Dal party.

## SAMPURNA VIKAS DAL

Sampurna Vikas Dal, a political party in the Indian state of Bihar. SVD was formed by ex-Rajya Sabha MP and former Rashtriya Janata Dal leader Ranjan Prasad Yadav on October 20, 2003. Yadav had differed with RJD leader Laloo Prasad Yadav when the latter appointed his wife, Rabri Devi, as the Chief Minister of the state.

# 4

# Language and Literature

## LANGUAGE

The term 'Hindi' is applied to two groups of dialects, viz. Western and Eastern. Western Hindi has four main dialects-Bundeli of Bundelkhand, Braj Bhasha of Mathura, Kanauji of Central Doab and Vernacular Hindusthani of Delhi and upper Doab. Eastern Hindi has three dialects namely Awadhi of Oudh, Begheli of Beghlkhand and Chattisgarhi of Chattisgarh. Eastern Hindi has Bihari to its east and Marathi to the south, both being outer languages.

Along with the above dialects, Hindi literature also includes the literatures of the parts of Rajasthan in the west and Bihari in the east which, strictly, are not Hindi at all. Thus the question arises, like other linguistic people of India, do the Hindi speaking people constitute a sub-nationality?

The question of Hindustani sub-nationality was raised as far back as 1922. Hindustani denotes the language of Hindustan and during the Muslim period, Hindustan was considered to be the north Indian geographical tract lying between the Punjab and Bengal, obviously this includes Bihar also. The failure to develop Hindustani sub-nationalism in contrast to Bengali and

Punjabi, Maharashtrian etc. was adduced to the lack of political consciousness.82 This is because while the regional elites were emerging in other areas, 'Hindustan' being the last citadel of moribund medieval feudalism, was cordoned off from the influence of modern ideas.

Being the main area of the upsurge of 1857, it invited the bloodiest reprisal and retribution and subsequently the deliberate negligence and indifference from the side of colonial rulers. As a result, strong feudal features survived here and in the entire Hindustani speaking area and thus leading to certain amount of isolation from as well as resistance to modernism.

Politically, Bihar was tagged to Bengal even during the pre-British days leading to her economic backwardness. On the other hand, culturally and linguistically being a part of the Hindi Heartland, she too smarted under relative conservatism.

While the social reform of various streams swept the three presidencies in spite of solid phalanx of orthodox opposition, the movement of Arya Samaj that found some following among the backward castes acted more as a vehicle of conservatism than regeneration.

In Bihar, the unit of social movement was caste, not village or region. Evidences of multi-castes reform movement are practically absent.

Against the background of the Bihar's economic backwardness, she developed a fragmented personality having a number of territorial entities with definite dialects like Bhojpuri, Magahi and Maithili, superimposed over a formidable hierarchy of caste system. Linguistically those dialects could be put into a common group known as 'Bihari languages'.

One can contest this classification but they are definitely distinct from Hindi and more related to Bengali, Assameese and Oriya, as all these dialects were derived from common root known as Ardha Magadhi Apabhransa. 'Like Bengali or Oriya, no common 'Bihari language has ever emerged.

## LANGUAGE AND LITERATURE

Languages of Bihar (2011)

Hindi (77.52%)

Maithili (12.55%)

Urdu (8.42%)

Other (1.51%)

Hindi is the official language of the state. Urdu is the second official language in 15 districts of the state. Maithili (including its dialect Bajjika), Bhojpuri, Angika and Magahi are also widely spoken in the state. Maithili is a recognised regional language of India under the Eighth Schedule to the Constitution of India.Bhojpuri and Magahi are sociolinguistically a part of the Hindi Belt languages fold, thus they were not granted official status in the state.

## BIHARI LITERATURE

In the field of literature, Bihar has produced a number of writers of Hindi, including Raja Radhika Raman Prasad Sinha, Acharya Ramlochan Saran, Acharya Shivpujan Sahay, Divakar Prasad Vidyarthy, Ramdhari Singh 'Dinkar', Ram Briksh Benipuri, Phanishwar Nath 'Renu', Gopal Singh "Nepali", Ramesh Chandra Jha and Baba Nagarjun. Writer and Buddhist scholar Mahapandit Rahul Sankrityayan was born in Uttar Pradesh but spent his life in the land of Lord Buddha, i.e., Bihar. Hrishikesh Sulabh is a short story writer, playwright and theatre critic. Arun Kamal and Aalok Dhanwa are poets.

### Other regional languages

Different regional languages also have produced some prominent poets and authors. Raza Naqvi Wahi was the preeminent Indian Urdu language poet during his time, was born in Khujwan, Siwan, Bihar, and wrote many Urdu Poetry and also awarded as Ghalib Award.

Sharat Chandra Chattopadhyay, writer in Bengali, resided for some time in Bihar. Indian writer in English Upamanyu Chatterjee also hails from Patna in Bihar. Devaki Nandan

Khatri, who at the beginning of the 20th century wrote novels including *Chandrakanta* and *Chandrakanta Santati*, was born in Muzaffarpur, Bihar. Vidyapati Thakur is the most renowned poet of Maithili. (c. 14–15th century).Usha Kiran Khan is a renowned Maithili writer.

Manoj Bhawuk is the most popular writer and poet of Bhojpuri language from Siwan, Bihar. He knows the pulse of rural-programming, and is currently working with Zee TV.

### *English*

- Satyapal Chandra has broken traditional stereotype in English literature by writing a number of English bestsellers of various genres
- Amitava Kumar - author, journalist, and professor of English at Vassar College. He was born in Arrah district in Bihar. Author of *Husband of a Fanatic*, *Bombay-London-New York*, and *Passport Photos*
- Siddhartha Chowdhury " Patna Roughcut", Diksha at St. Martin's, Day Scholar, Patna Manual of Style, Ritwik & Hriday
- R. K. Sinha - died in 2003. He was born in Munger district of Bihar. He was a gold medalist for his master of arts degree. He was awarded a D Phil from Oxford University in 1950
- Tabish Khair - poet and novelist, born in Gaya district of Bihar
- Uday Sahay "Making News, Media in Contemporary India (edited)" published by Oxford University Press, "Delhi, India in One City" published by Academic Foundation, and "Raj Bhavan of the Rising Arunachal Pradesh" published by SAUV Publication

### *Women Writers of English Literature*

- Nikita Singh - "Love @ Facebook
- Manna Bahadur *The Dance of Death* published by Penguin India March 2012

- Mallika Nawal *The Eleventh Commandment - An Introduction to Religio-Marketing* and *Religictionary - The A-Z of Religion* are international books. Her *Business Communication*, published by Cengage Learning is a leading management textbook that is prescribed at several universities including Jawaharlal Nehru Technological University, Hyderabad. Her debut novel *I'm a Woman & I'm on SALE* was released on 16 December 2013 and has been dedicated to Nirbhaya.

# 5

# Geography and Flora & Fauna

## STATE PROFILE

***Locationcation:*** Bihar is located in the eastern part of the country (between 83°-30' to 88°-00' longitude). It is an entirely landlocked state, although the outlet to the sea through the port of Kolkata is not far away.

Bihar lies midway between the humid West Bengal in the east and the sub humid Uttar Pradesh in the west which provides it with a transitional position in respect of climate, economy and culture. It is bounded by Nepal in the north and by Jharkhand in the south. The Bihar plain is divided into two unequal halves by the river Ganga which flows through the middle from west to east.

### Physical Features

| | |
|---|---|
| Latitude | 21°-58'-10" ~ 27°-31'-15" N |
| Longitude | 82°-19'-50" ~ 88°-17'-40" E |
| Rural Area | 92,257.51 sq. kms |
| Urban Area | 1,095.49 sq. kms |
| Total Area | 94,163.00 sq. kms |

| | |
|---|---|
| Height above Sea-Level | 173 Feet |
| Normal Rainfall | 1,205 mm |
| Avg. Number of Rainy Days | 52.5 Days in a Year |

## Administrative Units

| | |
|---|---|
| Divisions | 9 |
| Districts | 38 |
| Sub-Divisions | 101 |
| CD Blocks | 534 |
| Panchayats | 8,471 |
| Number of Revenue Villages | 45,103 |
| Number of Urban Agglomerations | 9 |
| Number of Towns | 130 |
| Statutory Towns | 125 |
| Non-Statutory Towns | 5 |
| Police Stations | 853 |
| Civil Police Stations | 813 |
| Railway Police Stations | 40 |
| Police Districts | 43 |
| Civil Police District | 39 |
| Railway Police District | 4 |

## Key Statistics - as per 2001 Census (Provisional)

| | |
|---|---|
| Population | 8,28,78,796 |
| Male | 4,31,53,964 |
| Female | 3,97,24,832 |
| Population (0~6 Years Group) | |
| In Absolute Numbers | 1,62,34,539 |
| | 83,75,532 |
| | 78,59,007 |
| Percentage of Total Population | 19.59% |
| | 19.41% |
| | 19.78% |

## SOIL AND CLIMATE OF BIHAR

### Soil

Soil is one of the most important resources of a nation. It is the gift of nature of immense value. The most common use of the word soil is in the sense of a medium in which plants grow, although it has a different connotation at different time and place, and for persons engaged in different professions. Almost all the economic activities are directly or indirectly dependent on soil. Thus soil is the backbone of agricultural and industrial development.

Soil has a number of characteristics, which may be regarded as the aggregate of the physical, chemical and biological properties. The Bihar plane consists of a thick alluvial mantle of drift origin overlying in most part. The siwalik and older tertiary rocks. The soil is mainly young loam rejuvenated every year by constant deposition of silt, clay and sand brought by different streams. This soil is deficient in phosphoric acid, nitrogen and humus, but potash and lime are usually present in sufficient quantity.

There are three major types of soil in Bihar:

- Piedmont Swamp Soil—found in northwestern part of west Champaran district.
- Terai Soil–found in northern part of the state along the border of Nepal.
- The Gangetic Alluvium – the plain of Bihar is covered by gangetic alluvium (both new as well as old).

## GEOGRAPHY OF BIHAR

Bihar is located in the eastern region of India between latitude 24°-20'-10" N ~ 27°-31'-15" N and longitude 83°-19'-50" E ~ 88°-17'-40" E. It is an entirely land–locked state, in a subtropical region of the temperate zone. Bihar lies between the humid West Bengal in the east and the sub humid Uttar Pradesh in the west, which provides it with a transitional position in respect of climate, economy and culture. It is bounded by Nepal in the north and by Jharkhand in the south. Bihar plain is divided into two unequal halves (North Bihar and South Bihar) by the river Ganges which flows through the middle from west to east. Bihar's land has average elevation above sea level of 173 feet.

## Political geography

The state is divided into 9 divisions and 38 districts, for administrative purposes.

## Geology

Bihar is in Indo-Gangetic plain so naturally fertile soil is one asset of the state. Thus Indo-Gangetic plain's soil is the backbone of agricultural and industrial development. The Indo-Gangetic plain in Bihar consists of a thick alluvial mantle of drift origin overlying in most part, the siwalik and older tertiary rocks. The soil is mainly little young loam rejuvenated every year by constant deposition of silt, clay and sand brought by streams but mainly by floods in Bihar

This soil is deficient in phosphoric acid, nitrogen and humus, but potash and lime are usually present in sufficient quantity. The most common soil in Bihar is Gangeticalluvium of Indo-Gangetic plain region, Piedmont Swamp Soil which is found in northwestern part of West Champaran district and Terai Soil which is found in northern part of Bihar along the border of Nepal. clay soil, sand soil and loamy soil are common in Bihar.

## GEOGRAPHY AND CLIMATE

Bihar has a diverse climate. Its temperature is subtropical in general, with hot summers and cool winters. Bihar is a vast stretch of fertile plain. It is drained by the Ganges River, including its northern tributaries Gandak and Koshi, originating in the Nepal Himalayas and the Bagmatioriginating in the Kathmandu Valley that regularly flood parts of the Bihar plains. The total area covered by the state of Bihar is 94,163 km (36,357 sq mi). the state is located between 24°-20'-10" N ~ 27°-

31'-15" N latitude and between 83°-19'-50" E ~ 88°-17'-40" E longitude. Its average elevation above sea level is 173 feet (53 m).

The Ganges divides Bihar into two unequal halves and flows through the middle from west to east. Other Ganges tributaries are the Son, Budhi Gandak, Chandan, Orhani and Phalgu. Though the Himalayas begin at the foothills, a short distance inside Nepal and to the north of Bihar, the mountains influence Bihar's landforms, climate, hydrology and culture. Central parts of Bihar have some small hills, for example the Rajgir hills. To the south is the Chota Nagpur plateau, which was part of Bihar until 2000 but now is part of a separate state called Jharkhand.

## GEOGRAPHICAL PLACES – DIGHWARA

There are several common temples of various Hindu deities. Also you can have a beautiful scene of sunset from the banks of Ganga.

***Around Dighwara:*** Around Dighwara, there are many small historical and sacred places, people from far and near come to visit these places.

***Temple of Maa Ambika, (Aami):*** This is a temple of goddess Durga's Ambika form. The temple is roughly 4km west from Dighwara town. It is made in an old fort like building on the banks of holy Ganga. The temple is an example of standard north Indian temple architecture. It has a central shrine called 'garvagriha', housing the main idol of goddess Ambika. There is a 'yagya kunda' where still religious acts are done. A large idol of Shiva has been erected recently near the yagya kunda.

***How to Reach?*** Dighwara can be reached by train or by road. Nearest railway junctions are Sonpur and Chapra. Nearest Airport is Chapra. International flights are from Patna.

## Dinapore

Dinapore was a British colony in Bihar. It is located on the bank of River Ganges, and is very near to Patna, the capital city of Bihar. After independence it has been a major cantt of the Indian army, currently it is known as Danapur, and it is still the place where one of the glorious regiments, the "Bihar Regiment" resides.

***Dinapur Cantonment:*** Dinapur Cantonment is a cantonment town in Patna District in the state of Bihar, India.

***Demographics:*** As of 2001 India census[GRIndia], Dinapur Cantonment had a population of 28,149. Males constitute 56% of the population and females 44%. Dinapur Cantonment has an average literacy rate of 71%, higher than the national average of 59.5%: male literacy is 77% and, female literacy is 63%. In Dinapur Cantonment, 13% of the population is under 6 years of age.

## Dinapur Nizamat

Dinapur Nizamat is a city and a municipality in Patna district in the state of Bihar, India.

***Demographics:*** As of 2001 India census[GRIndia], Dinapur Nizamat had a population of 130,339. Males constitute 53% of the population and females 47%. Dinapur Nizamat has an average literacy rate of 56%, lower than the national average of 59.5%: male literacy is 64% and, female literacy is 47%. In Dinapur Nizamat, 15% of the population is under 6 years of age.

***Divisions of Bihar:*** The state of Bihar in India is divided into 9 divisions as follows:

1. Patna Division
   - *Head Quarters:* Patna
   - *Districts (6 Nos):* Patna District; Nalanda District, also called Biharsharif District; Bhojpur District, also called Arrah District; Rohtas District, also called Sasaram District; Buxar District; Kaimur District, also called Bhabhua District.
2. Tirhut Division
   - *Head Quarters:* Muzaffarpur
   - *Districts (6 Nos):* West Champaran, also called Bettiah District; East Champaran, also called Motihari

District; Muzaffarpur District; Sitamarhi District; Sheohar District; Vaishali District, also called Hajipur District.

3. Saran Division
   - *Head Quarters:* Chapra
   - *Districts (3 Nos):* Saran District, also called Chapra District, Siwan District, Gopalganj District.
4. Darbhanga Division
   - *Head Quarters:* Darbhanga
   - *Districts (4 Nos):* Darbhanga District, Madhubani District, Samastipur District, Begusarai District.
5. Kosi Division
   - *Head Quarters:* Saharsa
   - *Districts (4 Nos) :* Saharsa District, Madhepura District, Supaul District.
6. Purnia Division
   - *Head Quarters:* Purnea
   - *Districts (4 Nos):* Purnia District, Katihar District, Araria District, Kishanganj District.
7. Bhagalpur Division
   - *Head Quarters:* Bhagalpur
   - *Districts (3Nos):* Bhagalpur District, Banka District, Navgachia District.
8. Munger Division
   - *Head Quarters:* Munger
   - *Districts (5 Nos):* Munger District, Jamui District, Khagaria District, Lakhisarai District, Sheikhpura District
9. Magadha Division
   - *Head Quarters:* Gaya
   - *Districts (5 Nos):* Gaya District, Nawada District, Aurangabad District, Jehanabad District, Arwal District

## Dumra, Sitamarhi

Dumra is a city and a notified area in Sitamarhi district in the state of Bihar, India.

***Geography:*** Dumra is located at 25.02° N 83.97° E. It has an average elevation of 86 metres (282 feet).

***Demographics:*** As of 2001 India census[GRIndia], Dumra had a population of 14,538. Males constitute 57% of the population and females 43%. Dumra has an average literacy rate of 77%, higher than the national average of 59.5%: male literacy is 80% and, female literacy is 73%. In Dumra, 11% of the population is under 6 years of age.

## Dumraon

Dumraon is a city and a municipality in Buxar district in the state of Bihar, India. Ustad Bismillah Khan, the shehnai maestro from India was born on March 21, 1916 at Bhirung Raut Ki Gali here.

***Geography:*** Dumraon is located at 25.55° N 84.15° E. It has an average elevation of 61 metres (200 feet). Dumraon is one of the oldest princely states in India.

***Demographics:*** As of 2001 India census[GRIndia], Dumraon had a population of 45,796. Males constitute 53% of the population and females 47%. Dumraon has an average literacy rate of 54%, lower than the national average of 59.5%: male literacy is 64% and, female literacy is 43%. In Dumraon, 17% of the population is under 6 years of age.

## Eksar

Eksar is a small village in the Chapra district of Bihar in India. This village is inhabited by 100 families and around 1000 people. It is 40 km from Chapra. Education system is fighting hard to survive, since it's facing government negligence.

The basic source of livelihood for people is farming and it is well known for rice, wheat and Mango orchids. Umashankar Singh is a well known personality of that village who served at Bokaro Steel City plant for more than 35 years and contributed to its growth over the years. His sons Sudeep Singh and Sujeet Singh are studying Masters in International Business.

This small village hold good for sight seeing and also religious temple.

## East Champaran

East Champaran is an administrative district in the state of Bihar in India. The district headquarters are located at Motihari.

The district occupies an area of 3969 km$^2$ and has a population of 3,933,636 (as of 2001). East Champaran is a part of Tirhut Division.

## Mehsi

Mehsi is the entry point of East Champaran connected with Rail and Road both. This small place has number of visiting places at the east side of Railway Station. Mirza Halim Shah mosque, dargah, A very old library 'Nagrik Pustakalaya', Old High school of English period, Orchards of Lichi and mangoes and other places of interest.

The basic lively-hood is agriculture and cottage industry.

The very famous cottage industry is for making Buttons from shells, sometimes referred to as mother-of-pearl (shell-a hard outer case of many molluscs, oyster — bivalve mollusc, esp. an edible kind, sometimes producing a pearl).

The shells are taken from rivers specially flowing through Eastern Uttar Pradesh.

The product, buttons and other ornamental pieces are sold in domestic and international market.

## Kesariya

Kesariya is in south east of the district and it famous for Kesariya Stupa locally known DEURA this is one of oldest stupa. It is also good for tourist particulary for Buddhist.

## Forbesganj

Forbesganj is a city and a municipality in Araria district in the state of Bihar, India.

***Geography:*** Forbesganj is located at 26.3° N 87.25° E. It has an average elevation of 46 metres (150 feet).

***Demographics:*** As of 2001 India census[GRIndia], Forbesganj had a population of 41,982. Males constitute 53% of the population and females 47%. Forbesganj has an average literacy rate of 61%, higher than the national average of 59.5%: male literacy is 67%, and female literacy is 54%. In Forbesganj, 16% of the population is under 6 years of age.

## Gamgaria Block

Gamgaria block is one of the administrative divisions of Madhepura district, Bihar state, India. The block has a population (2001 census) of 65,283. The block headquarters are located at a distance of 18 kms from the district headquarters, namely, Madhepura.

***Gandaki River:*** The Gandaki River, also known as the Kali Gandaki and the Gandak, is a tributary of the Ganges River. It rises in the Himalayas in the Mustang District region of Nepal, near the border with Tibet, where it is known as the Narayani.

It flows southward through a steep gorge known as the Kali Gandaki Gorge, between the mountains Dhaulagiri (8167 m) to the west and Annapurna (8091 m) to the east. South of the gorge the river makes a right-angle turn and runs east for a time until turning sharply to the southwest.

The river later curves back towards the southeast as it enters India. The river flows southwest across the Gangetic plain of Bihar state, eventually merging with the Ganges near at Hajipur Patna.

If one measures the depth of a canyon by the difference between the river height and the heights of the highest peaks on either side, the Kali Gandaki Gorge is the world's deepest.

The portion of the river between the Dhaulagiri and Annapurna massifs is at an elevation of between 1300 metres and 2600 metres, 5500 to 6800 metres lower than the two peaks.

In traditional and popular culture

- The Gandaki river is mentioned in the ancient Sanskrit epic Mahabharata.
- Episode 1 of "The Living Planet," David Attenborough's second nature documentary series, is set in the Kali Gandaki Gorge.

## JAMUI

Jamui district is one of the thirty-seven districts of Bihar state, India, and Jamui town is the administrative headquarters of this district. Jamui district is a part of Munger Division.

The district headquarters are located at Jamui. The district occupies an area of 3099 km² and has a population of 1,397,474 (as of 2001).

## Janakpur Road

Janakpur Road is a city and a notified area in Sitamarhi district in the Indian state of Bihar.

***Demographics:*** As of 2001 India census[GRIndia], Janakpur Road had a population of 13,341. Males constitute 53% of the population and females 47%. Janakpur Road has an average literacy rate of 64%, higher than the national average of 59.5%: male literacy is 72%, and female literacy is 55%. In Janakpur Road, 17% of the population is under 6 years of age.

## Jehanabad

Jehanabad is a city and a municipality in and the headquarters of Jehanabad district in the Indian state of Bihar. Earlier, Jehanabad was part of Gaya district. It is 50 km away from both Patna and Gaya.

***Demographics:*** As of 2001 India census[GRIndia], Jehanabad had a population of 81,723. Males constitute 54% of the population and females 46%.

Jehanabad has an average literacy rate of 63%, higher than the national average of 59.5%: male literacy is 70%, and female literacy is 54%. In Jehanabad, 16% of the population is under 6 years of age.

## JEHANABAD

Jehanabad District is one of the thirty-seven districts of Bihar state, India, and Jehanabad town is the administrative headquarters of this district. Jehanabad district is a part of Magadh Division.

***Area:*** 1,569 km?

***Population:*** Total: 1174900

***Rural:*** 1100430

***Urban:*** 74470

***Sub Divisions:*** Jehanabad

***Blocks:*** Ghosi, Jehanabad, Makhdumpur, Kako, Hulasganj

***Agriculture:*** Paddy, Wheat, Lentils

***Rivers :*** Phalgu

## Jhanjharpur

Jhanjharpur is a small town located on the bank of Kamla-Balan river under Madhubani district in Bihar. There are two important business hubs in the town: Jhanjharpur (R.S) Market, also known as New Market and Jhanjharpur Purani Bazar.

These markets are four kilometres apart. Sometimes the Kamla Balan river becomes curse for the town, frequently overflowing in July.This river is actually the amalgamation of two separate rivers, Kamla and Balan. A bridge passing over the river was constructed by the British before India's independence on 15 August 1947.

***Blocks:*** Jainagar, Pandaul, Rahika, Bisfi, Benipatti, Basopatti, Babubarhi, Rajnagar, Madhepur, Khutauna, Khajauli, Jhanjharpur, Ghoghardiha, Ladania, Madhwapur, Harlakhi, Laukahi, Andharatharhi, Lakhnaur, Phulparas, Andhrathadhi, Sahuria, Deohar, Shiba.

***Agriculture:*** Paddy, Wheat, Pea, Gram,

## Jogbani

Jogbani is a city and a notified area in Araria district in the Indian state of Bihar.

***Geography:*** Jogbani is located at 26.42° N 87.25° E. It has an average elevation of 67 metres (219 feet).

***Demographics:*** As of 2001 India census[GRIndia], Jogbani had a population of 29,962. Males constitute 53% of the population and females 47%. Jogbani has an average literacy rate of 37%, lower than the national average of 59.5%: male literacy is 47%, and female literacy is 26%. In Jogbani, 19% of the population is under 6 years of age.

## KAIMUR

Kaimur is an administrative district in the state of Bihar in India. The district headquarters are located at Bhabua. The district occupies an area of 3363 km² and has a population of 1,284,575 (as of 2001). A very large hilly and forest area, currently infested by bandits.

Kaimur district is a part of Patna Division.

***Headquarters:*** Bhabhua

***Population:*** Total: 983269

***Rural:*** 956228

***Urban:*** 27041

***Sub Divisions:*** Bhabhua, Mohania

***Blocks:*** Bhabhua, Ramgarh, Mohania, Durgawati, Adhaura, Bhagwanpur, Chand, Chainpur, Kudra, Rampur, Nuawon.

***Agriculture:*** Paddy Fields, Maize, Wheat, Sugar Cane

***Rivers:*** Karmnasha, Durgawati

## Kanti

Kanti is a city and a notified area in Muzaffarpur district in the Indian state of Bihar.

He is also a wellknown character in the Anime show FLCL

***Demographics:*** As of 2001 India census[GRIndia], Kanti had a population of 20,873. Males constitute 53% of the population and females 47%. Kanti has an average literacy rate of 48%, lower than the national average of 59.5%: male literacy is 57%, and female literacy is 38%. In Kanti, 17% of the population is under 6 years of age.

## Kasba (Purnia)

Kasba is a city and a notified area in Purnia district in the Indian state of Bihar.

***Demographics:*** As of 2001 India census[GRIndia], Kasba had a population of 25,522. Males constitute 53% of the population and females 47%. Kasba has an average literacy rate of 49%, lower than the national average of 59.5%: male literacy is 57%, and female literacy is 41%. In Kasba, 18% of the population is under 6 years of age.

## Kataiya

Kataiya is a city and a notified area in Gopalganj district in the Indian state of Bihar.

***Demographics:*** As of 2001 India census[GRIndia], Kataiya had a population of 17,896. Males constitute 52% of the population and females 48%. Kataiya has an average literacy rate of 42%, lower than the national average of 59.5%: male literacy is 53%, and female literacy is 30%. In Kataiya, 19% of the population is under 6 years of age.

# KATIHAR

Katihar District is one of the thirty-seven districts of Bihar state, India, and Katihar town is the administrative headquarters of this district. The district is a part of Purnia Division. The district occupies an area of 3056 km$^2$ and has a population of 2,389,533 (as of 2001).

***Headquarters:*** Katihar

***Area:*** 3,057 km?

***Population:*** Total: 1825380

***Rural:*** 1653761

***Urban:*** 171619

***Sub Divisions:*** Barsoi, Katihar Sadar, Manihari

***Blocks:*** Katihar, Barsoi, Kadwa, Amdabad, Manihari, Balrampur, Korha, Falka, Alamnagar, Barari, Pranpur, Mansahi, Samaeli, Kursaila, Hasanganj, Dandkhora

***Agriculture:*** Paddy, Makhana, Banana

***Industry:*** Jute and Paper Mills

***Rivers:*** Mahananda, Ganges, Koshi

***College:*** DS college katihar, KB jha college, Katihar Medical College and Hospital, MJM Mahila College, Katihar.

***High Schools :*** Katihar High School, Adarsh High School, Maheshwary Academy, Marwari Pathshala, Gandhi High School, BMP

## KHAGARIA

Khagaria District is one of the thirty-seven districts of Bihar state, India, and Khagaria town is the administrative headquarters of this district. Khagaria district is a part of Munger Division.

***Headquarters:*** Khagaria

***Area:*** 1,486 km?

***Population:*** Total: 987227

***Rural:*** 928423

***Urban:*** 58804

***Sub Divisions:*** Khagaria, Ghoghri

***Blocks:*** Gogarı, Parwatta, Khagaria, Alauli, Chautham, Beldaur, Mansi.

***Agriculture:*** Paddy, Wheat, Maize, Jute

***Rivers:*** Ganges, Kosi, Budhi Gandak, Bagmati, Kamla Balan, Kali Kosi, Kareh

Khagaria is an administrative district in the state of Bihar in India. The district headquarters are located at Khagaria. The district occupies an area of 1486 $km^2$ and has a population of 1,276,677 (as of 2001). The district is surrounded by seven rivers namely Ganga, Kamla Balan,Koshi, Budhi Gandak, Kareh, Kali Koshi and Bagmati. These rivers cause floods every year. Khagaria is small town with a major railway junction on the Barauni Guwahati section of the Indian Railways. National Highway no 31 which connects rest of India to North Eastern region passes through this town.

It is also connected to other regions of north Bihar by another rail line to Saharsa and Samastipur. Building of a major rail bridge across river Ganga is underway to connect it to south Bihar and Jharkhand directly.

***History:*** Also known as Farakiya in local region. There is an interesting story behind it. Five centuries ago Akbar, then king of Mughal empire directed his revenue minister Todarmal to map his entire empire. But he could not map this region now known as Khagaria due to difficult terrain, rivers and dense forests. So he named it Farakiya (Farak in Hindi means separate). Now there is even a weekly newspaper- 'Farkiyanchal Times'.

***People and Culture:*** Predominantly a rural district it has a colourful culture. Major festivals are Chat Pooja, Holi, Durga Pooja and Dipawali. People here tend to marry within their region only. You will find quite soft spoken and mild mannered people contrary to the general perception about Bihar.

Majority of population of Khagaria town is of younger age signifying a shifting population from villages to district centre. Doordarshan, the national television broadcaster has one local broadcasting centre here.

## Language and Dialects

***Education:*** Major educational centres are located in the town of Khagaria. Besides many govt. run schools there is one prestigious centre for higher education Koshi College, Khagaria. DAV public school Khagaria has constantly ranked among the top schools of Bihar.

Majority of students after finishing higher secondary go to other big cities like Patna or Delhi for higher education. District has a distinct reputation for producing IAS officers constantly. Many students from here are now settled abroad and doing great.

***Economy:*** Agriculture is the backbone of rural economy here. Land is fertile providing major farm output. SUDHA milk cooperative Federation runs a milk pasteurising and packaging unit here. Landscape is picturesque covered by orchards, farms, rivers, swamps and forests. If properly developed it can be a big tourist attraction in future.

## Khagaul

Khagaul is a city and a municipality in Patna district in the Indian state of Bihar.

***Geography:*** Khagaul is located at 25.58° N 85.05° E. It has an average elevation of 55 metres (180 feet).

***Demographics:*** As of 2001 India census[GRIndia], Khagaul had a population of 48,330. Males constitute 53% of the population and females 47%. Khagaul has an average literacy rate of 71%, higher than the national average of 59.5%: male literacy is 77%, and female literacy is 65%. In Khagaul, 13% of the population is under 6 years of age.

## Kharagpur (Munger)

Kharagpur is a city and a notified area in Munger district in the Indian state of Bihar.

***Geography:*** Kharagpur is located at 25.12° N 86.55° E. It has an average elevation of 48 metres (157 feet).

***Demographics:*** As of 2001 India census[GRIndia], Kharagpur had a population of 26,910. Males constitute 53% of the population and females 47%.

Kharagpur has an average literacy rate of 47%, lower than the national average of 59.5%: male literacy is 55%, and female literacy is 39%. In Kharagpur, 18% of the population is under 6 years of age.

## Khusrupur

Khusrupur is a city and a notified area in Patna district in the Indian state of Bihar.

***Demographics:*** As of 2001 India census[GRIndia], Khusrupur had a population of 12,185. Males constitute 53% of the population and females 47%. Khusrupur has an average literacy rate of 54%, lower than the national average of 59.5%: male literacy is 62%, and female literacy is 45%. In Khusrupur, 17% of the population is under 6 years of age.

# KISHANGANJ

Kishanganj district is one of the thirty-seven districts of Bihar state, India, and Kishanganj town is the administrative headquarters of this district. Kishanganj district is a part of Purnia division.

***Koath:*** Koath is a city and a notified area in Rohtas district in the Indian state of Bihar.

Koath is famous for its unique sweet-dish called Belgrami.

***Geography:*** Koath is located at 25.32° N 84.27° E. It has an average elevation of 73 metres (239 feet).

***Demographics:*** As of 2001 India census[GRIndia], Koath had a population of 15,809. Males constitute 52% of the population and females 48%. Koath has an average literacy rate of 48%, lower than the national average of 59.5%: male literacy is 59%, and female literacy is 36%. In Koath, 19% of the population is under 6 years of age.

## Koilwar

Bold text SONE" is the river flowing by the side of this village. This village also has a steel rail road bridge made before independence. The bridge is shown in the famous film: GANDHI: also. The water of the river sone is still quenching the thirst of a lot of villagers. This village also has a renowned TB hospital. Koilwar is a city and a notified area in Bhojpur district in the Indian state of Bihar.

***Demographics:*** As of 2001 India census[GRIndia], Koilwar had a population of 19,925. Males constitute 61% of the population and females 39%. Koilwar has an average literacy rate of 55%, lower than the national average of 59.5%: male literacy is 55%, and female literacy is 54%. In Koilwar, 19% of the population is under 6 years of age.

## Kosi Division

Kosi Division division is an administrative geographical unit of Bihar state of India. Saharsa is the administrative headquarters of the division. Currently (2005), the division consists of Saharsa district, Madhepura district, and Supaul district.

## Kumarkhand Block

Kumarkhand block is one of the administrative divisions of Madhepura district, Bihar state, India. The block has a population (2001 census) of 187,030. The block headquarters are located at a distance of 29 km from the district headquarters, namely, Madhepura.

## Lakhisarai

Lakhisarai is a city and a municipality in Lakhisarai district in the Indian state of Bihar.

***Demographics:*** As of 2001 India census[GRIndia], Lakhisarai had a population of 77,840. Males constitute 53% of the population and females 47%. Lakhisarai has an average literacy rate of 50%, lower than the national average of 59.5%: male literacy is 59%, and female literacy is 39%. In Lakhisarai, 18% of the population is under 6 years of age.

## Lalganj

Lalganj is a city and a municipality in Vaishali district in the Indian state of Bihar.

***Geography:*** Lalganj is located at 25.87° N 85.18° E. It has an average elevation of 42 metres (137 feet).

***Demographics:*** As of 2001 India census[GRIndia], Lalganj had a population of 29,847. Males constitute 52% of the population and females 48%. Lalganj has an average literacy rate of 51%, lower than the national average of 59.5%: male literacy is 60%, and female literacy is 42%. In Lalganj, 18% of the population is under 6 years of age.

## Lauria Nandan Garh

Lauria Nandan Garh is a village about 14 km from Shikarpur and 24 km from Bettiah in the state of Bihar in northern India. Here there are interesting ruins of a huge stupa. It is a 26 metre high ancient brick sepulchral mound thought to be the stupa where the ashes of Lord Buddha were enshrined.

Less than half a kilometer from the village, stands the famous pillar of Ashoka. It is a single block of polished sandstone over 32 feet (10 m) high. The top is bell shaped with a circular abacus ornamented with Brahmi geese supporting the statue of a lion.

The pillar is inscribed with the edict of Ashoka in clear and beautifully cut characters. The lion has been chipped in the month and the column bears the mark of time just below the top which has itself been slightly dislodged.

## Lauthaha

Lauthaha is a city and a notified area in Purba Champaran district in the Indian state of Bihar.

***Demographics:*** As of 2001 India census[GRIndia], Lauthaha had a population of 7744. Males constitute 63% of the population and females 37%. Lauthaha has an average literacy rate of 75%, higher than the national average of 59.5%: male literacy is 78%, and female literacy is 70%. In Lauthaha, 10% of the population is under 6 years of age.

## Lodipur

Lodipur is a small village in Konch subdivision of Gaya District in the state of Bihar, India. It is about 6 km from

Tekari, located on a state highway. Most of the people are from Hindu community but some Muslim people also live here in harmony with all. It has about 80% litteracy and may be called a model village on that account.

## MADHEPURA

Madhepura district is one of the thirty-seven districts of Bihar state, India, and Madhepura town is the administrative headquarters of this district. Madhepura district is a part of Kosi division.

Madhepura is an administrative district in the state of Bihar in India. The district headquarters are located at Madhepura. The district occupies an area of 1787 km$^2$ and has a population of 1,524,596 (as of 2001). Madhepura district is surrounded by Araria and Supaul district in the north, Khagaria and Bhagalpur district in the south, Purnia district in the east and Saharsa district in the West. It is situated in the Plains of River Koshi and located in the Northeastern part of Bihar at longitude between 25°. 34 to 26°.07' and latitude between 86° .19' to 87°.07'.

## MADHUBANI

Madhubani District is one of the thirty-seven districts of Bihar state, India, and Madhubani town is the administrative headquarters of this district. Madhubani district is a part of Darbhanga Division.

The district occupies an area of 3501 km$^2$ and has a population of 3,570,651 (as of 2001). This is the centre of Mithila, a region where the main language is Maithili. The "Madhubani" style of paintings derives its name from this region as the style originated here, in the early 17th century. These paintings are made using vegetable dyes, and the canvas is usually cloth or paper.

These days, several of the well-known "Mahubani" paintings are used as motifs on bags, kurtas ( an Indian garment for covering the upper-half of the body), and other materials produced using the hand-block painting technique. With ethnic-chic being in vogue, such products are all the rage, these days, not just with the Indians, but also in the export market.

***Population:*** Total: 361687 Rural: 351921 Urban: 9766

***Sub Divisions:*** Madhubani, Jaynagar, Benipatti, Jhanjharpur, Phul Paraas

***Blocks:*** Jainagar, Pandaul, Rahika, Bisfi, Benipatti, Basopatti, Babubarhi, Rajnagar, Madhepur, Khutauna, Khajauli, Jhanjharpur, Ghoghardiha, Ladania, Madhwapur, Harlakhi, Laukahi, Andharatharhi, Lakhnaur, Phulparas

***Agriculture:*** Paddy.

***Industry:*** Sugar factories, Pisciculture.

***Rivers:*** Kamala and Bhutahi Balaan.

## Magadha Division

Magadha division is an administrative geographical unit of Bihar state of India. Gaya is the administrative headquarters of the division. Currently (2005), the division consists Gaya district, Nawada district, Aurangabad district, Jehanabad district, and Arwal district.

## Maharajganj

Maharajganj is a city and a notified area in Siwan district in the Indian state of Bihar.

***Geography:*** Maharajganj is located at 26.12° N 84.48° E. It has an average elevation of 66 metres (216 feet).

***Demographics:*** As of 2001 India census[GRIndia], Maharajganj had a population of 20,878. Males constitute 50% of the population and females 50%. Maharajganj has an average literacy rate of 50%, lower than the national average of 59.5%: male literacy is 61%, and female literacy is 40%. In Maharajganj, 19% of the population is under 6 years of age.

## Maner

Maner is a city and a notified area in Patna district in the Indian state of Bihar.

***Geography:*** Maner is located at 25.65° N 84.88° E. It has an average elevation of 54 metres (177 feet).

***Demographics:*** As of 2001 India censusGRIndia, Maner had a population of 26,912. Males constitute 53% of the population and females 47%. Maner has an average literacy rate of 52%, lower than the national average of 59.5%: male literacy is 61%, and female literacy is 42%. In Maner, 19% of the population is under 6 years of age.

## Marhaura

Marhaura is a city and a notified area in Saran district in the Indian state of Bihar.

***Geography:*** Marhaura is located at 25.97° N 84.87° E. It has an average elevation of 52 metres (170 feet).

***Demographics:*** As of 2001 India censusGRIndia, Marhaura had a population of 24,534. Males constitute 52% of the population and females 48%.

Marhaura has an average literacy rate of 42%, lower than the national average of 59.5%: male literacy is 54%, and female literacy is 29%. In Marhaura, 19% of the population is under 6 years of age.

## Mokameh

Mokameh is a city and a municipality in Patna district in the Indian state of Bihar.

***Demographics:*** As of 2001 India censusGRIndia, Mokameh had a population of 56,400. Males constitute 53% of the population and females 47%. Mokameh has an average literacy rate of 56%, lower than the national average of 59.5%: male literacy is 65%, and female literacy is 47%. In Mokameh, 16% of the population is under 6 years of age.

## Motipur

Motipur is a city and a notified area in Muzaffarpur district in the Indian state of Bihar.

***Demographics:*** As of 2001 India censusGRIndia, Motipur had a population of 21,933. Males constitute 53% of the population and females 47%. Motipur has an average literacy rate of 43%, lower than the national average of 59.5%: male literacy is 52%, and female literacy is 33%. In Motipur, 19% of the population is under 6 years of age.

## MUNGER DISTRICT

Munger District is one of the thirty-seven districts of Bihar state, India, and Munger town is the administrative headquarters of this district. Munger district is a part of Munger Division.

***Population:*** Total: 943583

***Rural:*** 660418

***Urban:*** 283165

***Sub Divisions:*** Haveli Kharagpur, Munger, Tarapur

***Blocks:*** Haveli, Kharagpur, Dharhara, Munger, Jamalpur, Tarapur, Sangrampur, Bariarpur, Tetiabamber, Asarganj

***Agriculture:*** Paddy, Wheat, Lentils

***Industry:*** ITC cigarette plant, Gun Factory

***Rivers:*** Ganges, Mohane, Harohar, Kiul

***History:*** Munger, spelled Monghyr throughout British rule, is one of the most historic towns of Bihar. Known to be ruled by Karna, Its ruler Mir Kasim fought one of the last battles before East India Company captured the eastern India. The Fort built by him has three gates and Ganga on its four sides. Currently Munger hosts one of the biggest Yoga centres of the world ?Bihar School of Yoga? that offers postgraduate courses as well.

The District of Monghyr has an area of 3922 sq. M. The Ganges divides it into two portions. The northern, intersected by the Burhi Gandak and Tiljuga, two important tributaries of the Ganges, is always liable to inundation during the rainy season, and is a rich, flat, wheat and rice country, supporting a large population. A considerable area, immediately bordering the banks of the great rivers, is devoted to permanent pasture. Immense herds of buffaloes are sent every hot season to graze on these marshy prairies; and the ghi, or clarified butter, made from their milk forms an important article of export to Calcutta.

To the south of the Ganges the country is dry, much less fertile, and broken up by fragmentary ridges. Irrigation is necessary throughout the section lying on the south of the Ganges. The population in 1901 was 2,068,804, showing an increase of 1.6% in the decade. The principal exports sent to Calcutta, both by rail and by river, are oil-seeds, wheat, rice, indigo, grain and pulse, hides and tobacco; and the chief imports consist of European piece-goods, salt and sugar.

The southern portion of the district is well provided with railways. At Lakhisarai junction the arc and chord lines of the East Indian railway divide, and here also starts the branch to Gaya. At Jamalpur, which is the junction for Monghyr, are the engineering workshops of the company. In the early years of British rule Monghyr formed a part of Bhagalpur, and was not created a separate district till 1832.

## Background Information of District

Munger is so located in the southern part of Bihar and its headquarters is located at the southern part of the Ganges. It lies between 24°20' and 25°30' N latitude and 85°37' to 87°30' E longitude. Height from sea level is 30 to 65 m. It is divided into three subdivisions, namely Munger Kharagpur and Tarapur. There are nine development blocks - Munger, Jamalpur, Bariyarpur, Dharhara, Kharagpur, Tetiabambar, Tarapur, Asarganj and Sangrampur.

***Climate:*** There are three distinct seasons in this zone. Summer (March to May), monsoon (June to September) and winter (October to February). Average annual rainfall of this district is 1146 mm (53 yr avg).

***The District:*** The district occupies an area of 1419 km$^2$ and has a population of 1,135,499 (as of 2001).

## Munger Division

Munger division is an administrative geographical unit of Bihar state of India. Munger is the administrative headquarters of the division. Currently (2005), the division consists of Munger District, Jamui District, Khagaria District, Lakhisarai District, and Sheikhpura District.

## Muzaffarpur

The town of Muzaffarpur famous for Litchis (a fruit found only in a few locations in the world) is a vibrant city of North Bihar situated on the bank of Himalaya snow-fed perennial river Burhi/Budhi ( Old ) Gandak. Muzaffarpur pronunciationis an administrative district in the state of Bihar in India.

The district headquarters are located at Muzaffarpur. The district occupies an area of 3173 km$^2$ and has a population of 3,743,836 (as of 2001).Mark Twain, while on way to Kathmandu, stayed in the local Muzaffarpur Club and relished this beautiful East Indian town.

Muzaffarpur is a leading centre of education in Bihar. It boasts of a medical and an engineering college (S.K.Medical College(1969) and Muzaffarpur Institute of Technology (1954)) and one of the oldest universities of North Bihar (Bihar University, now known as B R A Bihar University). Langat Singh College affiliated to the University of Bihar had the likes of Dinkar (a famous Hindi poet), Dr. Rajendra Prasad (the first president of India), and Acharya J. B. Kriplani as its faculty members.

It is also famous for sugar cane and the district has a few sugar mills - now old and dilapidated. It had been the commercial hub of North Bihar and the wholesale centre of all types of mill clothes in famous Marwari community dominated Suta Patti and Commodities in "Gola" Market of Saraiyagunj. Muzaffarpur is a rapidly growing city. The population explosion in the last decade has been phenomenal. Thousands of villagers migrated to this town from nearby villages in the rapid uncontrolled urbanization in post-independence India. However, this has led to a host of problems, the most prominent of them being drainage and sanitation.

Due to the topography of the city (the central parts of the city are lower than the outer areas), drainage has always been a problem area. In recent years this has been greatly compounded by the population explosion, lack of quality engineering and technological expertise, and most notably, due to extremely poor governance, inefficiency, rampant corruption, problems with policing and law and order, and lack of work culture at many levels of the government machinery.

The downtown area of Muzaffarpur is known as Kalyani Chowk and Saraiyagunj. Both areas are densely populated with small shops selling a plethora of goods and services, with colourful settings and buzzing with large crowds. Motijheel is a place where all things are found. There are many shops selling a variety of goods. Chakkar maidan is a place where there is small settlement of the Indian army & nearby are popular schools like Prabhat Tara . Popular temples are Kali temple , Garib Sthan ( Shiva Temple) Devi Mandir Durga. Apart from these ,there are several old temples in the town.

***Climate:*** The summer is extremely hot and humid (40 deg C,90 % Max.) and winters are pleasnat ( 6 deg C ).There are few historical places to visit nearby such as Vaishali (claimed as first-ever Democratic State in the world ) and one of the place ( of Buddhism and Jainism Importance- 35 km.). Outing- Flood plains in green settings dotted with sweet water ponds ,meandering glacier fed rivulets and innumerable fruit orchards are ideal for picnics. The city has a water table just 20 ft. below the ground and is green round the year. Hotels -There area few hotels with A.C. and non-A.C.rooms .

## Educational Institutions

(1) *Muzaffarpur Institute of Technology:* This is among the engineering institutions coming just after the independence (in 1954). The foundation stone of this institute was laid by first Prime Minister of India Jawahar

Lal Nehru. It is one of the 'reputed' institutions of Bihar having a very beautiful campus.

MIT offers UG courses in Civil Engineering, Mechanical Engineering, Electrical Engineering, Electronics & Communication engineering, Information Technology, Leather Technology and Pharmacy.

Its alumni hold responsible positions (some of them have reached top positions) in government, public sector and private sector organizations in India and abroad.

(2) S.K. Medical College

(3) *B.R.A. Bihar University:* This is the oldest university of north Bihar having crumbling buildings in sync with general state of affairs of Bihar.

(4) *Langat Singh College:* This the oldest college of Muzaffarpur.

(5) *M.D.D.M. College:* "Mahant Darshan Das Mahila College".

(6) R.D.S. College

(7) R.M.L College This college is named after Dr. Ram Manohar Lohia.

(8) S.A.V. School

## NAWADA

Nawada is a city and a municipality in and headquarters of Nawada district in the Indian state of Bihar.

***Geography:*** Nawada is located at 24.88° N 85.53° E. It has an average elevation of 80 metres (262 feet). Kakolat Fall is a popular fall in Bihar. Many people come for picnics from different places in India in the summer season. It is 20KM far from Nawada.

***Demographics:*** As of 2001 India censusGRIndia, Nawada had a population of 82,291. Males constitute 53% of the population and females 47%. Nawada has an average literacy rate of 65%, higher than the national average of 59.5%: male literacy is 71%, and female literacy is 59%. In Nawada, 16% of the population is under 6 years of age.

## Nawada

Nawada district is one of the thirty-seven districts of Bihar state, India, and Nawada town is the administrative headquarters of this district. Nawada district occupies an area of 2492 km$^2$ and has a population of 1,809,425 (as of 2001). Headquarters: Nawadah.

***Area:*** 2,494 km?

***Population:*** Total: 1359694

***Rural:*** 1265138

***Urban:*** 94556

***Sub Divisions:*** Nawadah, Rajauli

***Blocks:*** Kauakol, Varsaliganj, Nawadah, Rajouli, Akbarpur, Hisua, Narhat, Govindpur, Pakribarawan, Sirdalla, Kasichak, Roh, Nardiganj, Meskaur

***Agriculture:*** Paddy

***Industry:*** Bidi factories

***Rivers:*** Sakri

## Odantapuri

Odantapuri, also called Uddandapura, was a Buddhist vihara in what is now Bihar, India. It was built by king Dharmapala of Pala dynasty in the 8th century.

## PATNA

Patna district is one of the districts of Bihar state, India, with Patna as the district headquarters. Patna district is a part of Patna division.

***Headquarters:*** Patna

***Area:*** 3202 km$^2$

***Population:*** Total: 36,23,225

***Rural:*** 22,41,510

***Urban:*** 11,19,800

***Sub Divisions:*** (6 Nos) : Patna Sadar, Patna City, Barh, DanaPur, Masaurhi, Paliganj

***Blocks:*** Patna Sadar, Phulwari sharif, Sampatchak, Fatuha, Khusrupur, Daniyawaan, Barh, Bakhtiarpur, Belchi, Athmalgola, Mokama, Pandarak, Ghoswari, Bihta, Maner, Danapur, Naubatpur, Masaurhi, Dhanarua, Punpun

***Agriculture:*** Paddy, Maize, Pulses and Wheat. Also oil seeds. Roughly one third of the area sown is under rice (paddy). Cash crops such as vegetables and water-melons are also grown in Diara belt

## Industry: Leather, Handicrafts, Agro Processing

***Rivers:*** Ganga, Sone, Punpun Colleges: Maulana Azad College of Engineering & Technology (MACET), National Institute of Technology(NIT), Patna Medical College and Hospital, Patna Women's College, J D Women's College, Magadha Mahila College, Arvind Mahila college, Science College, Patna College, B N College, Commerce College, A N College, College of Commerce, Nalanda Medical College and Hospital.

***Schools:*** Mount Carmel, St. Joseph's Convent, Notredam academy, Bankipur girls high school, Don Bosco Academy, Delhi Public School, D A V, Kendriya Vidyalaya, St. Xaviers.

## Patna Division

Patna division is an administrative geographical unit of Bihar state of India. Patna is the administrative headquarters of the division. Currently (2005), the division consists Patna District; Nalanda District, also called Biharsharif District; Bhojpur District, also called Arrah district; Rohtas District, also called Sasaram district; Buxar District; Kaimur District, also called Bhabhua district.

## Phulwari Sharif

Phulwari Sharif is a city and a notified area in Patna district in the Indian state of Bihar.

***Demographics:*** As of 2001 India censusGRIndia, Phulwari Sharif had a population of 53,166. Males constitute 53% of the population and females 47%. Phulwari Sharif has an average literacy rate of 63%, higher than the national average of 59.5%: male literacy is 70%, and female literacy is 56%. In Phulwari Sharif, 15% of the population is under 6 years of age.

## Purnia Division

Purnia division is an administrative geographical unit of Bihar state of India. Purnia is the administrative headquarters of the division. Currently (2005), the division consists of Purnia district, Katihar district, Araria district, and Kishanganj district.

***Rajgir Hills:*** Rajgir hills, lying in central regions of Bihar state, India, are two parallel ridges extending around 65 km. The highest point in the hills rise to an altitude of 388 meters, but mostly the hills are around 300 meters high. Between these two ridges lie a number of places of historical importance, dating from the period of the Mahabharatha, Gautam Buddha, Mahavira, Mauryas and the Guptas. Currently, Rajgir is the most famous place of the area.

## Raxaul

Raxaul is a town in northern India, only 2 kilometres from the border with Nepal and near the Nepalese town of Birganj. Raxaul is a sub-divisional town in the East Champaran district of Bihar and is an Indian customs point. The popular village in Raxaul is Pachori Tola about 6 kilometers from Raxaul Bazar. This information is written and edited by Vikash Kumar (Handi Bazar, Raxaul).

***Raxaul Bazar:*** Raxaul Bazar is a city and a municipality in Purbi Champaran district in the Indian state of Bihar.

***Demographics:*** As of 2001 India censusGRIndia, Raxaul Bazar had a population of 41,347. Males constitute 54% of the population and females 46%. Raxaul Bazar has an average literacy rate of 58%, lower than the national average of 59.5%: male literacy is 66%, and female literacy is 48%. In Raxaul Bazar, 18% of the population is under 6 years of age. The Most Popular of Village is : (1) Raghunathpur (Pachori Tola) (Village of Raxaul MLA Dr. Ajay Singh, Govt Teacher Sri Kedar Nath Pachori) (2) Gamhariya (3) chainpur (4) charwa.

## Revelganj

Revelganj is a city and a municipality in Saran district in the Indian state of Bihar.

***Geography:*** Revelganj is located at 25.78° N 84.67° E. It has an average elevation of 52 metres (170 feet).

***Demographics:*** As of 2001 India censusGRIndia, Revelganj had a population of 34,044. Males constitute 52% of the population and females 48%. Revelganj has an average literacy rate of 45%, lower than the national average of 59.5%: male literacy is 56%, and female literacy is 32%. In Revelganj, 17% of the population is under 6 years of age.

## ROHTAS

Rohtas district is one of the thirty-seven districts of Bihar state, India, and Sasaram town is the administrative headquarters of this district. Rohtas district is a part of Patna Division. The distrist has an area of 3850 $km^2$, a population of 2,448,762 (2001 census), and a population of 636 persons per $km^2$.

## Rosera

Rosera is a city and a municipality in Samastipur district in the Indian state of Bihar.

***Demographics:*** As of 2001 India censusGRIndia, Rosera had a population of 27,494. Males constitute 53% of the population and females 47%. Rosera has an average literacy rate of 57%, lower than the national average of 59.5%: male literacy is 65%, and female literacy is 47%. In Rosera, 18% of the population is under 6 years of age.

## SIWAN

Siwan is one of the districts of Bihar state, India, and Siwan town is the administrative headquarters of this district. Siwan district is a part of Saran Division.

***Area:*** 2,219 $km^2$

***Population:*** Total: 2170971

***Rural:*** 2055466

***Urban:*** 115505

***Sub Divisions:*** Siwan, Maharajganj

***Blocks:*** Mairwa, Pachrukhi, Raghunathpur, Aandar, Guthani, Maharajganj, Darauli, Siswan, Daraunda, Husainaganj, Bhagwanpur, Hat, Goriyakothi, Baraharia, Siwan Sadar, Basantpur, Lakari, Nabiganj, Jiradei, Nautan, Hasanpur.

***Agriculture:*** Paddy, Wheat, Sugar Cane

***Industry:*** Sugar factories, Thread factories

***Rivers:*** Daha, Jharhi, Gandak and Ghaghara, Daha River which flows through Siwan

Siwan is the district headquarters of the Siwan district in the Indian state of Bihar.

***Geography:*** Siwan (the old name Alipur) is located at 25.13° N 83.88° E. It has an average elevation of 77 metres (252 feet).

***Demographics:*** As of 2001 India censusGRIndia, Siwan had a population of 108,172. Males constitute 53% of the population and females 47%. Siwan has an average literacy rate of 63%, higher than the national average of 59.5%: male literacy is 69%, and female literacy is 55%. In Siwan, 15% of the population is under 6 years of age.

## Sonpur

Sonpur is a town in the Indian state of Bihar, that is situated on the banks of the River Gandak in Saran district in the Indian state of Bihar.

***Geography:*** It is located at 25.7° N 85.1833° E at an altitude of 42 metres (137 feet). It is the divisional headquarters of the East Central Railway of the Indian Railways.

It hosts one of the world's largest animal fairs. Of the seven railway stations in the world having the longest railway platforms, as many as five are in India, Sonepur being the one with the longest platform in the world (2,415 feet).

***Demographics:*** As of 2001 India censusGRIndia, Sonpur had a population of 33,389. Males constitute 53% of the population and females 47%.

Sonepur has an average literacy rate of 60%, higher than the national average of 59.5%: male literacy is 70%, and female literacy is 48%. In Sonepur, 16% of the population is under 6 years of age.

## Sugauli

Sugauli is a city and a notified area in East Champaran district in the Indian state of Bihar.

***Demographics:*** As of 2001 India censusGRIndia, Sugauli had a population of 31,362. Males constitute 54% of the population and females 46%. Sugauli has an average literacy rate of 42%, lower than the national average of 59.5%: male literacy is 51%, and female literacy is 32%. In Sugauli, 20% of the population is under 6 years of age.

## Sultanganj

Sultanganj is a city and a notified area in Bhagalpur district in the Indian state of Bihar.

***Demographics:*** As of 2001 India censusGRIndia, Sultanganj had a population of 41,812. Males constitute 54% of the population and females 46%. Sultanganj has an average literacy rate of 52%, lower than the national average of 59.5%: male literacy is 60%, and female literacy is 43%. In Sultanganj, 17% of the population is under 6 years of age.

## Supaul

Supaul is a city and a municipality in Supaul district in the Indian state of Bihar. Supaul district occupies an area of 2410 km$^2$ and has a population of 1,745,069 (as of 2001).

***Geography:*** Supaul is located at 25.93° N 86.25° E. It has an average elevation of 34 metres (111 feet).

***Demographics:*** As of 2001 India censusGRIndia, Supaul had a population of 54,020. Males constitute 53% of the population and females 47%. Supaul has an average literacy rate of 49%, lower than the national average of 59.5%: male literacy is 59%, and female literacy is 38%. In Supaul, 18% of the population is under 6 years of age.

### SUPAUL

Supaul district is one of the thirty-seven districts of Bihar state, India, and Supaul town is the administrative headquarters of this district. Supaul district is a part of Kosi division.

## Tarapur

Tarapur is a small town in the district of Munger in the Indian state Bihar. It is connected by road to most important towns in Bihar. The nearest railway station is Sultanganj. The main occupation of people residing around Tarapur is agriculture. Paddy, wheat, pulses, sugarcane, and other cereals are grown here. Mango from this region is also famous. Tarapur has been growing as an administrative unit as well as a commercial centre in Munger.

During *shrawani mela*, a month long religious carnival where devotees go to the historic Shiva temple in Deoghar after taking the water from the "utrawahini" Ganga in Sultanganj, the whole locality is decked like a bride.

People from Tarapur are spread all over India and in different places of the globe. Many prominent personalities were born in Tarapur. From the village of Maheshpur near Tarapur, we had former minister the late Mrs. Sumitra Devi, pracharak of Vedas Dr. Singeshwar Prasad Singh, and the former Head of the Art department of Banaras Hindu University, Varanasi the late Dr. Brahmdeo Madhur.

## Tekari

Tekari is a city and a municipality in Gaya district in the Indian state of Bihar. Maharaja Gopalsaran was the king of this area in accident times. The fort is still there. It is a place of tourist's interest. Late Prof. Naresh Pd Singh (S.N.Sinha college) belong to this holy place. Some of the nearby villages are Jalalpur (Tekari), Lodipur, Chiraali etc.

***Geography:*** Tekari is located at 24.93° N 84.83° E. It has an average elevation of 82 metres (269 feet).

***Demographics:*** As of 2001 India censusGRIndia, Tekari had a population of 17,615. Males constitute 52% of the population and females 48%. Tekari has an average literacy rate of 66%, higher than the national average of 59.5%: male literacy is 74%, and female literacy is 57%. In Tekari, 17% of the population is under 6 years of age.

## Thakurganj

Thakurganj is a city and a notified area in Kishanganj district in the Indian state of Bihar.

***Geography:*** Thakurganj is located at 26.45° N 88.13° E. It has an average elevation of 82 metres (269 feet).

***Demographics:*** As of 2001 India censusGRIndia, Thakurganj had a population of 15,288. Males constitute 53% of the population and females 47%. Thakurganj has an average literacy rate of 54%, lower than the national average of 59.5%: male literacy is 63%, and female literacy is 44%. In Thakurganj, 17% of the population is under 6 years of age.

## Tirhut

Historically Tirhut refers to the Indo-Gangetic plains lying north of the Ganga River, in the Indian state of Bihar. The geographical area known as Tirhut corresponds to the ancient region of Mithila. Tirhut, a densely populated area of India, has alluvial plains and several rivers pass through these plains. The main crops include paddy, wheat, maize, and sugarcane. Some regions of Tirhut, particularly around Muzaffarpur and Hajipur are respectively renowned for Litchi and bananas. In ancient time, the area was part of the kingsom of Vaishali.

During the initial period of the British Raj, Tirhut district was formed in 1873, as part of Patna division. Tirhut district was thereafter reorganized into two districts, namely, Darbhanga and Muzaffarpur.

In 1908, Tirhut was carved out of Patna division to form a new division named Tirhut division, a name which still (2005) continues, but the boundaries have changed several times due to reorganization of districts and creating smaller districts over decades. Originally, Tirhut division consisted of five districts: Darbhanga , Muzaffarpur, Saran, East and West Champaran.

During the 19th and early 20th century, Tirhut region was an important place for Indigo plantation and processing. Mahatma Gandhi started his Satyagraha movement from areas around, Motihari, which was part of Tirhut. Currently, Indigo plantation and processing has since become extinct in this region.

## Tirhut Division

Tirhut division is an administrative geographical unit of Bihar state of India. Muzaffarpur is the administrative headquarters of the division. Currently (2005), the division consists of West Champaran, also called Bettiah district; East Champaran, also called Motihari district; Muzaffarpur district; Sitamarhi district; Sheohar district; Vaishali district, also called Hajipur district.

## Udakishunganj Block

Udakishunganj block is one of the administrative divisions of Madhepura district, Bihar state, India. The block has a population (2001 census) of 136,842.

The block headquarters are located at a distance of 35 km from the district headquarters, namely, Madhepura.

### SAMASTIPUR

Samastipur District is one of the thirty-seven

***Districts of Bih:*** *134877*

***Sub Divisions:*** Dalsinghsarai, Patori, Rosera, Samastipur Sadar

***Blocks:*** Jitwarpur, Kalyanpur, Warisnagar, Rosara, Tajpur, Morwa, Patori, Sarairanjan, Pusa, Ujiyarpur, Dalsinghsarai, Singhia, Hasanpur, Musrigharari, Mohiuddinnagar, Bibhutipur, Bithan, Shivajinagar, Vidyapatinagar, Khanpur, Mohanpur

***Institutes:*** Agricultural university pusa, '*J.N.V. Birauli*'

***Agriculture:*** Paddy, Maize

***Industry:*** Sugar factories, Paper mill, Jute mill.

***Rivers:*** Budhi Gandak, Kamala, Balaan

## Saran Division

Saran division is an administrative geographical unit of Bihar state of India. Chapra is the administrative headquarters of the division. Currently (2005), the division consists of Saran District, also called Chapra District, Siwan District, Gopalganj District.

## Sasaram

Sasaram (sometimes also spelled as Sahsaram) is the administrative headquarters of Rohtas district in the Indian state of Bihar.

***History:*** It is an ancient city and is believed to derive its name from Sahasrabahu, an ancient king and Parsuram, the warrior sage. Sasaram is also famous for the red sandstone mausoleum of Emperor Sher Shah Suri, built during 1540-45 AD stands magnificently in the middle of an artificial lake.

***Geography:*** Sasaram is located at 24.95° N 84.03° E. It has an average elevation of 101 metres (331 feet). Sasaram Railway station is located on the Grand Chord line of the Indian Railways, connecting Calcutta and Delhi. The famed Grand Trunk Road passes through Sasaram town.

***Demographics:*** As of 2001 India censusGRIndia, Sasaram had a population of 131,042. Males constitute 53% of the population and females 47%. Sasaram has an average literacy rate of 65%, higher than the national average of 59.5%: male literacy is 72%, and female literacy is 58%. In Sasaram, 16% of the population is under 6 years of age.

***Economy:*** It also has a fertile agricultural hinterland.

## Shahabad

Shahabad, with headquarters at Arrah was one of the districts of Bihar, India. The district was subsequently bifurcated into a number of districts. Kunwar Singh belonged to this district.

## Shahpur

Shahpur is a city and a notified area in Bhojpur district in the Indian state of Bihar.

***Geography:*** Shahpur is located at 25.58° N 84.45° E. It has an average elevation of 51 metres (167 feet).

***Demographics:*** As of 2001 India censusGRIndia, Shahpur had a population of 14,456. Males constitute 52% of the population and females 48%. Shahpur has an average literacy rate of 47%, lower than the national average of 59.5%: male literacy is 58%, and female literacy is 34%. In Shahpur, 19% of the population is under 6 years of age.

## Sheikhpura

Sheikhpura is a city and a municipality in Sheikhpura district in the Indian state of Bihar. Sheikhpura is also an administrative district in the state of Bihar in India. The district occupies an area of 689 km$^2$ and has a population of 525,137 (as of 2001).

***Demographics:*** As of 2001 India censusGRIndia, Sheikhpura had a population of 43,042. Males constitute 53% of the population and females 47%. Sheikhpura has an average literacy rate of 51%, lower than the national average of 59.5%: male literacy is 60%, and female literacy is 42%. In Sheikhpura, 18% of the population is under 6 years of age.

## Sheohar

Sheohar is a city and a notified area in and headquarters of Sheohar district in the Indian state of Bihar.

***Geography:*** Sheohar is located at coor 26.52N, 85.3E. It has an average elevation of 53 metres (173 feet).

***Demographics:*** As of 2001 India censusGRIndia, Sheohar had a population of 21,327. Males constitute 53% of the population and females 47%. Sheohar has an average literacy rate of 35%, lower than the national average of 59.5%: male literacy is 44%, and female literacy is 25%. In Sheohar, 20% of the population is under 6 years of age.

## SHEOHAR

Sheohar is an administrative district in the state of Bihar in India. The district headquarters are located at Sheohar, and the district is a part of Tirhut Division. This district was carved out of Sitamarhi district in 1994.

The district occupies an area of 443 $km^2$ and has a population of 514,288 (as of 2001).

This district has mixed population of Hindus and Muslims. Agriculture is the main stay. It is one of the most flood affected district in Bihar. Dekuli is a holy place popular for ancient temple of lord Shiva.

***River:*** Bagmati.

***Population:*** Total: 377699

***Rural:*** 363784

***Urban:*** 13915

***Blocks:*** Sheohar, Tariyani, Piprahi, Dumri-katsari.

## Silao Nalanda

Silao is a city and a notified area in Nalanda district in the Indian state of Bihar. It is known for the excellent Khaja made by its Halwais. It is also the head quarters of a Block, a small administrative unit, by the same name.

***Geography:*** Silao is located at 25.08° N 85.42° E. It has an average elevation of 60 metres (196 feet).

***Demographics:*** As of 2001 India censusGRIndia, Silao had a population of 20,177. Males constitute 52% of the population and females 48%. Silao has an average literacy rate of 52%, lower than the national average of 59.5%: male literacy is 60%, and female literacy is 43%. In Silao, 19% of the population is under 6 years of age.

## SITAMARHI

Sitamarhi is one of the districts of Bihar state, India, and Sitamarhi town is the administrative headquarters of this district. Sitamarhi district is a part of Tirhut Division.

***Population:*** Total: 2013796

***Rural:*** 1894203

***Urban:*** 119593

***Sub Divisions:*** Sitamarhi Sadar, sheohar, Pupri

***Blocks:*** Bathnaha, Parihar, Nanpur, Bazpatti, Bairgania, Belsand, Riga, Sursand, Pupri, Sonbarsa, Dumra, Runni Saidpur, Majorganj, Puranhia, Suppi, Parsauni, Bokhra, Chorout

***Agriculture:*** Paddy, Wheat, Maize, Lentils

***Industry:*** Sugar Factory, Rice and Oil Mills.

***Rivers:*** Bagmati

***History:*** This is the place where Sita was born, the main character of the epic Ramayana. The town is situated along the border of Nepal. The district of Sitamarhi was carved out of Muzaffarpur district on 11th December 1972. It is situated in the northern part of Bihar. Its headquarter is located at Dumra, five kilometers south of Sitamarhi.

Sitamarhi is a sacred place in Hindu mythology. Its history goes back to Treta Yug. Sita, the wife of Lord Rama sprang to life out of an earthern pot, when Raja Janak was ploughing the field somewhere near Sitamarhi to impress upon Lord Indra for rain. It is said that Raja Janak excavated a tank at the place where Sita emerged and after her marriage set up the stone figures of Rama, Sita and Lakshman to mark the site. This tank is known as Janaki-kund and is south of the Janaki Mandir.

In course of time, the land lapsed into a jungle until about 500 years ago, when a Hindu ascetic, named Birbal Das came to know the site by divine inspiration.

He came down from Ayodhya and cleared the jungle. He found the images set up by Raja Janak, built a temple over there and commenced the worship of Janaki or Sita. The Janaki Mandir is apparently modern and is about 100 years old only. The town however contains no relics of archaeological interest.

It has witnessed communal violence lead by local politicians in the past but on the whole both the leading communities here a good rapport. This district is often bereaved by natural calamities. One of the most devastating is excess flooding due to mismanagement of the banks by both civilians and government officials.

***Head Quarters:*** Sitamarhi

***Population:*** Total: 2013796

***Rural:*** 1894203

***Urban:*** 119593

***Sub Divisions:*** Sitamarhi Sadar, Pupri

***Blocks:*** Bairgania, Bajpatti, Bathnaha, Belsand, Parihar, Nanpur, Riga, Sursand, Pupri, Sonbarsa, Dumra, Runni Saidpur, Majorganj, Suppi, Parsauni, Bokhra, Chorout.

***Villages:*** Ratwara, Bela, Madhopur, Amanpur, Rudauli, Boha, Rasalpur, Paktola

***Agriculture:*** Paddy, Wheat, Maize, Lentils

***Industry:*** Sugar Factory, Rice and Oil Mills.

***Rivers:*** Bagmati, Lakhandei

***Sports:*** Heman Trophy (cricket) is organised every year at the Goinka College Grounds, which adds some zeal to the life of the youths. Cricket is played in every nook and corner of the district.

***Festivals:*** Durga puja, Vishwakarma puja, Sarswati puja and other festivals are celebrated with great enthusiasm.

## FLORA OF BIHAR

The Indian state of Bihar contains sub-Himalayan foothills and mountains with moist deciduous forests. Rainfall may exceed 1600 millimeters per year. Common trees include *Shorea robusta* (*sal*), *Toona ciliata*, *Diospyros melanoxylon* (*kendu*), *Boswellia serrata* (*salai*), *Terminalia tomentosa*(*asan*), *Terminalia bellirica* (*bahera*), *Terminalia arjuna* (*arjun*), *Pterocarpus marsupium* (*paisar*), *Madhuca indica* (*mahua*).

## FAUNA OF BIHAR

The Ganges River dolphin, or "susu" occur in the Ganges and Brahmaputra, south Asia's largest river systems. It can now be considered amongst the most endangered mammals of the region.

The Ganges River dolphin ranges from 2.3 to 2.6 meters in length. The tail fluke is on average 46 cm in width. Females are larger than males. The color of this dolphin varies from lead-colored to black. The undersides are lighter in color. The rostrum is 18 to 21 cm in length and the forehead is steep and rises abruptly from the base of the snout.

The dorsal fin is rudimentary and ridge-like, and the ends of the pectoral fins are squared instead of tapered. The neck is visibly constricted and the blowhole is a longitudinal slit. There are 28 to 29 teeth on either side of the jaw. The eye and optic nerve of the Ganges river dolphin are degenerate. The eye lacks a lens and is therefore incapable of forming images on the retina. However, it functions in light-detection. It is believed that the lack of a true visual apparatus in the river dolphin is related to its habitat; the water in which it lives is so muddied that vision in essentially useless.

Valmiki National Park, West Champaran district, covering about 800 km$^2$ of forest, is the 18th Tiger Reserve of India, and is ranked fourth in terms of density of tiger population. It has diverse landscapes, sheltering rich wildlife habitats and floral and faunal composition, with the prime protected carnivores.

## FLORA AND FAUNA

*Bauhinia acuminata, locally known as* Kachnaar

Bihar has notified forest area of 6,764.14 km (2,612 sq mi), which is 7.2% of its geographical area. The sub Himalayan foothill of Someshwar and the Dun ranges in the Champaran district are another belt of moist deciduous forests. These also consist of scrub, grass and reeds. Here the rainfall is above 1,600 millimetres (63 in) and thus promotes luxuriant Sal forests in the area. The most important trees are Shorea Robusta, Sal Cedrela Toona, Khair, and Semal. Deciduous forests also occur in the Saharsa and Purnia districts. Shorea Robusta (sal), Diospyros melanoxylon (kendu), Boswellia serrata (salai), Terminalia tomentose (Asan), Terminalia bellerica (Bahera), Terminalia Arjuna (Arjun), Pterocarpus Marsupium (Paisar), Madhuca indica (Mahua) are the common flora across the forest of Bihar.

Valmiki National Park, West Champaran district, covering about 800 km (309 sq mi) of forest, is the 18th Tiger Reserve of India and is ranked fourth in terms of density of tiger population. It has a diverse landscape, sheltering rich wildlife habitats and floral and faunal composition, along with the prime protected carnivores.

## NATURAL RESOURCES

Bihar lies in the tropical to sub tropical region. Rainfall here is the most significant factor in determining the nature of vegetation. Bihar has a monsoon climate with an average annual rainfall of 1200 mm.

## Forests

The sub Himalayan foothills of Someshwar and Dun ranges in Champaran constitute another belt of moist deciduous forests. This also consists of scrub, grass and reeds. Here the rainfall is above 1,600 mm and thus promotes luxuriant Sal forests in the favoured areas.

The hot and dry summer gives the deduous forests. The most important trees are Shorea Robusta (Sal), Shisham, Cedrela Toona, Khair, and Semal. This type of forests also occurs in Saharasa and Purnia districts.

## Fertile Land

The topography of Bihar can be easily described as a fertile alluvial plain occupying the Gangetic Valley. The plain extends from the foothills of the Himalayas in the north to a few miles south of the river Ganges as it flows through the State from the west to the east. Rich farmland and lush orchards extend throughout the state. Following are the major crops: paddy, wheat, lentils, sugarcane, jute (hemp, related to the marijuana plant, but a source of tough fibers and "gunny bags"). Also, cane grows wild in the marshes of West Champaran. The principal fruits are: mangoes, banana, jack fruit and litchis. This is one the very few areas outside China which produces litchi.

## Water Resources

Water like ground and mineral resources is of great significance as it provides means of drinking water for man and animals, irrigation for agriculture, industrial uses, production of hydro-electricity, transportation and recreation etc. The importance of water is so immense that the people in ancient times worshipped it. Bihar is richly endowed with water resources, both the ground water resource and the surface water resource. Not only by rainfall but it has considerable water supply from the rivers which flow within the territory of the State. Ganga is the main river which is joined by tributaries with their sources in the Himalayas. Some of them are Saryu (Ghaghra), Gandak, Budhi Gandak, Bagmati, Kamla-Balan and Mahananda.

There are some other rivers that start from the platue area and meet in Ganges or its associate rivers after flowing towards north. Some of them are Sone, Uttari Koyal, Punpun, Panchane and Karmnasha.

There are several rivers in Bihar which contribute a lot to the peoples of Bihar. These rivers make the water available for irrigation purpose and also help in generating the hydro-thermal energy for the state. Apart from this they provide a medium for water transport, provide fishes for fishery industry and enrich the natural resources of state in many other ways. All the above rivers have their impact on the Bihar plain. State also has non-exhaustible source of ground water which is in use for drinking purposes, irrigation and industries.

## Mineral Production

| | | |
|---|---|---|
| Steatite | - | 945 Tonnes |
| Pyrites | - | 9,539 Tonnes |
| Quartzite | - | 14,865 Tonnes |
| Crude Mica | - | 53 Tonnes |
| Limestone | - | 4,78,000 Tonnes |

The clickable map shown below allows you to find out the basic information about any specific district of Bihar. Alternatively, you can also make use of the links of individual districts.

## WILDLIFE

The history of wildlife in Bihar commences with the legislation of Private Forests Act which restricted the Zamindar's ownership of forests. Thus, the government acquired 26,000 square kilometres of jungle which was fast being wiped out of its fauna. Today, Bihar boasts of 2 national parks and 21 sanctuaries which includes the country's only hideout for wolves; a sanctuary for dolphins; a crocodile centre; a welcome jheel, receptive to lakhs of birds migrating from Central Asia, besides other surprises lurking from the priceless heritage of the wild denizens.

## Valmiki National Park

Valmiki National Park (335 sq. km) has been created amidst 544 sq. km of Valmiki Sanctuary in the West Champaran district of Bihar, bordering Nepal. The magnificent Himalayan hills offer a relatively cooler and more picturesque hideouts to enjoy the bounties of nature. Adjacent to the sanctuary, in the forests of Nepal is the historic Valmiki Ashram amidst Chitwan National Park of Nepal.

One horned rhinoceros and Indian bison often migrate from Chitwan to Valmikinagar. The forest of the sanctuary is rich in Bhabar-Dun sal, dry Siwalik sal, khair, cane etc. Tigers dominate the wildlife scene while other attractions include Chittals, Sambhars, Nilgais, Leopards, Hyenas, Indian civets, Jungle cats, Hog deer and Wild dogs. Valmikinagar ranks fourth as far as the density of tiger population is concerned.

## Hazaribagh Wildlife Sanctuary

107 km from Ranchi. The best time to visit is February-March and October-November. Known for its Sal forested hills, tiger, sambar, nilgai, cheetal, leopard etc. It is situated 16 km from Hazaribagh. Set in hilly terrain, the park is a Tiger Project Reserve and is a part of the Chotta Nagpur plateau in tribal territory. Its 186 sq. km is forested with grass meadows and some deep waterways The best time to visit is Feb-Apr. The park supports nilgai, deer, leopard, tiger, sambar, wild boar, chital and wild cat. There are 10 watchtowers and hides for viewing.

## Palamau Tiger Reserve

180 km from Ranchi. It is also known as the Belta National Park, in the Chotta Nagpur Plateau, the park covers the area of 930 sq. km of dry deciduous forest, mainly of sal and bamboo. Although it is open throughout the year yet the best time to visit is Oct-Nov. It is the second major wildlife sanctuary in

Bihar which was once the home of the extinct Indian cheetah.

This place is famous for its forested hills, tiger, leopard, elephant, sambar, jungle cat, rhesus macaque (monkey) and occasionally wolf. The wildlife also includes gaur, nilgai, Indian wolf and many species of birds. Over 200 species of water, woodland birds and hot springs add to interests.

## Dalma Wildlife Sanctuary

10 km from Jamshedpur. The best time to visit is October-June. It is the best elephant habitat of Bihar, where the pachyderms love to spend their summer. Unlike Palamu reeling under scorching sun, Dalma continues to be pleasing with temperatures under 30 degrees C. The availability of water during summer is all the more alluring for the elephants to migrate.

## Koderma Wildlife Sanctuary

Koderma Wildlife Sanctuary (177 sq. km) situated on Patna-Ranchi highway. Besides its rich wildlife the place is famous for its numerous scenic spots. The most popular being Fhwajadhari Hillock.

## Kaimur wildlife Sanctuary

Kaimur wildlife Sanctuary (1342 sq. km.) is the largest and one of the best faunal areas of the state, rich in black bucks and nilgais. Other wildlife denizens include chinkaras, tigers, leopards, hyenas, sloth bears, etc.

## Bhimbandh Sanctuary

(682 sq. km) close to Bhagalpur is another home to a variety of wildlife. Besides tiger, panther, wild boar, sambhar, chittals and nilgai, the forests here are famous for hot water springs which are said to contain traces of radio active materials.

## Jaivik Udyan (Zoological Garden)

Jaivik Udyan (Zoological Garden) is about 16km from Ranchi town on Ranchi - Patna road near Ormanjhi, is the zoological garden named Jaivik Udyan. A number of mammalian faunas have been collected there for visitors gaiety.

## Other Wildlife Sanctuaries

Lawalong Wildlife Sanctuary - which is 100 km from Gaya.

The best time to visit is October-June.

Rajgir Wildlife Sanctuary—102 km from Patna.

The best time to visit is October-June.

Topchanchi Wildlife Sanctuary —100 km from Dhanbad.

The best time to visit is October-June.

Kabar Lake Bird Sanctuary—22 km from Begusarai.

The best time to visit is November-March.

# 6

# Economy

## INTRODUCTION

Bihar is the fastest growing state in terms of gross state domestic product (GSDP), clocking a growth rate of 17.06% in FY 2014–15.

The economy of Bihar was projected to grow at a compound annual growth rate (CAGR) of 13.4% during 2012–2017, i.e. the 12th Five-Year Plan.

Bihar has witnessed strong growth in per capita net state domestic product (NSDP). At current prices, per capita NSDP of the state grew at a CAGR of 12.91 per cent during 2004–05 to 2014–15. Bihar's per capita income went up by 40.6 per cent in the financial year 2014–15.

| Year | Gross State Domestic Product (millions of Indian Rupees) |
|---|---|
| 1980 | 73,530 |
| 1985 | 142,950 |
| 1990 | 264,290 |
| 1995 | 244,830 |
| 2000 | 469,430 |
| 2005 | 710,060 |

*Bihar accounts for 71% of India's annual litchiproduction.*

*A village market*

Gross state domestic product of Bihar for the year 2013/2014 has been around 3683.37 billion INR. By sectors, its composition is:

Agriculture = 22%

Industry = 5%

Services = 73%.

## Agriculture

Bihar is the fourth-largest producer of vegetables and the eighth-largest producer of fruits in India. Bihar has high agricultural production making it one of the strongest sectors of the state. About 80 per cent of the state's population is employed in agriculture, which is higher as compared to India's average. The main agricultural products produced in Bihar are litchi, guava, mango, pineapple, brinjal, lady's finger, cauliflower, cabbage, rice, wheat and sugarcane and sunflower. Though good soil and favourable climatic conditions such as good rainfall favour agriculture, it has to encounter flood threat as well, which may drain off the fertile soil, if not conserved properly. The state (mostly southern parts) faces droughts almost every year affecting production of crops such as paddy.

## Industry

Bihar has emerged as brewery hub with major domestic and foreign firms setting up production units in the state. Three major firms – United Breweries Group, Danish Brewery Company Carlsberg Group and Cobra Beer – are to set up new units in Patna and Muzaffarpur in 2012.

Hajipur, near Patna, remains a major industrial city in Bihar, linked to the capital city through the Ganges bridge and good road infrastructure.

The state's debt was estimated at 77% of GDP by 2007. The Finance Ministry has given top priority to create investment opportunities for big industrial houses like Reliance Industries. Further developments have taken place in the growth of small industries, improvements in IT infrastructure, the new software park in Patna, Darbhanga, Bhagalpurand the completion of the expressway from the Purvanchal border through Bihar to Jharkhand. In August 2008, a Patna registered company called the Security and Intelligence Services (SIS) India Limited took over the Australian guard and mobile patrol services business of American conglomerate, United Technologies Corporation (UTC). SIS is registered and taxed in Bihar. The capital city, Patna, is one of the better-off cities in India when measured by per capita income.^ The State Government is setting up an Information Technology (IT) City at Rajgir in Nalanda district. Additionally, India's first Media Hub is also proposed to be set up in Bihar.

## Income distribution

In terms of income, the districts of Patna, Munger, and Begusarai were the three best-off out of a total of 38 districts in the state, recording the highest per capita gross district domestic product of 31,441, 10,087 and 9,312, respectively, in 2004–05.

### THE ECONOMIC STRANGULATION

Simple economic logic tells us that a region falling way behind needs greater investment in its development. But Bihar is being systematically denied even its rightful due from the Centre, let alone the additional assistance its economic and social condition deserves. If the present state of affairs continues, it will only imperil India, for the country cannot really progress without Bihar's advancement, say Mohan Guruswamy and Abhishek Kaul.

That Bihar is India's poorest and most backward State is undeniable. The facts speak for themselves. But what makes its situation unique is that Bihar is the only State where poverty levels are uniformly at the highest level (46-70 per cent) in all the sub-regions. The annual real per capita income of Bihar — Rs 3,650 — is about a third of the national average of Rs 11, 625. Bihar is also the only State where the majority of the population — 52.47 per cent — is illiterate.

But Bihar has its bright spots. Its infant mortality rate is 62 per 1,000, which is below the national average of 66 per 1,000. But what is interesting is that this is better than not just UP (83) and Orissa (91), but better even than States such as AP and Haryana (both 66).

Even in terms of life expectancy, the average Bihari male lives a year longer (63.6 yrs.) than the average Indian male (62.4 yrs) and the State's performance in increasing life spans has been better than most in the past three years.

Bihar has 7.04 million hectares under agriculture and its yield of 1,679 kg per hectare, while less than the national average of 1,739 kg per hectare, is better than that of six other States, including some big agricultural States like Karnataka and Maharashtra. Despite this, in socio-economic terms at least, Bihar is clearly in terrible shape.

Bihar is not only the worst off of all Indian States, but the gap between it and the rest is also widening. But there is another reality as well. It is that India cannot progress without Bihar's advancement. It is much too big to be left behind.

Even after Jharkhand was taken out of it, Bihar still has a population of about 85 million. But more relevant than that, for policy purposes, is that Bihar has India's largest concentration in the below 25 years age cohort, with 58 per cent in this category. It will retain this position till well into this century, which means that as India ages, Bihar will remain young! And what the young need most is health, education and jobs. Or else.

Thus, the development of Bihar is integral to India's development. India cannot go forward leaving Bihar behind. This is not the time to apportion blame for Bihar's plight. But that it is in this condition is a severe indictment of our national leadership that has so blatantly and wilfully ignored the Bihar economic problem.

The successive State Governments too are equally culpable. Who is more responsible for this is a chicken-or-egg question? It does not matter now. But one thing is clear. Bihar has few willing to speak up for it. The numbers are proof of its systematic and deliberate neglect.

As opposed to an All-India per capita developmental expenditure (from 2000 to 2002) of Rs 6748.50, Bihar's is less than half at Rs 3,206.00.

While development expenditure depends on a bunch of factors, including a State's contribution to the national exchequer, no logic can explain away the per capita Tenth Plan size which, at Rs 2533.80, is less than a third of that of States such as Gujarat (Rs 9,289.10), Karnataka (Rs 8,260.00) and Punjab (Rs 7,681.20).

Simple and sound economic logic tells us that when a region is falling way behind, it calls for a greater degree of investment in its progress and development. It is analogous to giving a weak or sick child in the family better nutrition and greater attention. Only in the animal kingdom do we see the survival of the fittest, with the weak and infirm neglected, deprived and even killed.

But Bihar is being systematically denied, let alone the additional assistance its economic and social condition deserves, but also what is its rightful due. From the pitiful per capita investment in Bihar, it is obvious that the Central Government has been systematically starving Bihar of funds.

One can understand that the share in Central taxation is determined by the formula of the Finance Commission that takes into account the contribution of an individual State to the exchequer. But one is hard put to understand why this inequality, and such a glaring inequality, should extend to grants, special assistance and even to Plan allocations.

That politics has a lot to do with neglect is seen from the fact that while AP received Rs 3,507.60 crore (1998 to 2000) as "additional Central assistance for externally-aided projects in State Plans," Bihar received just Rs 306.90 crore.

Even in terms of grants from the Central Government (2000 to 2002), Bihar fares poorly. It received Rs 4,047.30 crore while AP topped the list with Rs 9,790.00 crore. Bihar has also been neglected as far as net loans from the Centre are concerned. It received just Rs 2,849.60 as against Rs 6,902.20 received by AP from 2000-02. It is only in terms of per capita share of central taxes do we see Bihar getting its due.

This gross neglect by the Central government is reflected in the low per capita Central assistance (additional assistance, grants and net loans from the Centre) received by Bihar in 2001. While AP received Rs 625.60 per capita, Bihar got a paltry Rs 276.70.

The results of the economic strangulation of Bihar can be seen in the abysmally low investments possible in the State government's four major development thrusts. Bihar's per capita spending on roads is Rs 44.60, just 38 per cent of the national average of Rs 117.80.

Similarly, for irrigation and flood control, Bihar spends just Rs 104.40 on a per capita basis as opposed to the national average of Rs 199.20.

Despite this, Bihar manages a few sunshine pictures. Its per capita spending on education, at Rs 484.10, is as good as the best. AP spends Rs 493.90 and the national average is Rs 586.8.

But in terms of per capita expenditure on medical and public health, Bihar falls well behind with Rs 86.20, against the national average of Rs 157.20.

Despite this its infant mortality rate (62 per 1,000) is better than the national average (66 per 1,000). Not only is this better than the other Bimaru States but it is also better than Andhra Pradesh, which stands at 66 per 1,000.

The World Bank's country study of India's poverty actually shows that the change in Bihar's social infrastructure has been the highest in India, while economic deterioration has been among the lowest.

Now, the question of how much did Bihar "forego"? If Bihar got just the All-India per capita average, it would have got Rs 48,216.66 crore for the Tenth Five Year Plan instead of the Rs 21,000.00 crore it has been allocated. It would have got Rs 44,830 crore as credit from banks instead of the Rs 5,635.76 crore it actually got, if it were to get the benefit of the prevalent national credit/deposit ratio.

Similarly, Bihar received a pittance from the financial institutions, a mere Rs 551.60 per capita, as opposed to the national average of Rs 4,828.80 per capita. This could presumably be explained away by the fact that Bihar now witnesses hardly any industrial activity. But no excuses can be made for the low investment by NABARD.

On a cumulative per capita basis (2000 to 2002) Bihar received just Rs 119.00 from NABARD as against Rs 164.80 by AP and Rs 306.30 by Punjab. It can be nobody's argument that there is no farming in Bihar.

If the financial institutions were to invest in Bihar at the national per capita average, the State would have got Rs 40, 020.51 crore as investment instead of just Rs 4,571.59 crore that it actually received.

Even if with the wave of some magic wand the inequities of the past are wiped away, it is doubtful that Bihar can absorb such huge sums in the near future. For a start it just doesn't have the administrative wherewithal to use the money productively. But the present state of affairs cannot continue. If they do, it only imperils India, for already we can see a gathering storm of red terror over a wide arc from Nepal to Chattisgarh, with Bihar in the middle of it.

Quite clearly Bihar is not only being denied its due share, but there is a flight of capital from Bihar, India's poorest and most backward State. This is a cruel paradox indeed. The cycle then becomes vicious.

This capital finances economic activity in other regions, leading to a higher cycle of taxation and consequent injection of greater Central government assistance there. If one used harsher language one can even say that Bihar is being systematically looted, just as the British looted India. Criticism of Bihar's political elite and its polity that has become a standard feature of our national discourse has only served as a smokescreen to deny the State its rightful due.

## ECONOMIC CONSTRAINTS

To understand the economic backwardness and non-development of subnationalism in Bihar, history obviously steps into the area of investigation because the probe is conducted in terms of time. But space too is relevant here, because the former is not only a chronological phenomenon (a dialogue between the past and present) but also, if spatially denoted a dialogue between part and whole. Thus our quest runs correspondingly through several digits of part and whole of India and Bihar and other Indian union.

During the national movement, specially during the Gandhian era, Bihar was in the forefront. But the spell of nationalistic spirit did not give rise to industrial entrepreneurship. At the same time, anti-feudal movement of the period led by Kisan Sabhas intensified agro-entrepreneurship. This phenomenon has peculiar interrelationship with the caste factor of Bihar with corresponding political implications as pointed above.

The question arises why Bihar could not evolve regional industrial entrepreneurship despite great nationalistic spirit. In relation to the concept of Protestant ethics, it is often posed : is it not a little artificial to suggest that the capitalist enterprise has to wait till some religious or other spirit has produced capitalist spirit.

On the other hand, question can also be put: can the whole edifice of industrial entrepreneurship develop without the corresponding growth of material forces. Hence the problems in relation to Bihar are (1) why nationalism couldn't give rise to entrepreneurship, and (2) why material forces for capitalistic enterprise could not develop here.

Post-independence India has witnessed systematic attempt at planned economic development in the country as a whole. Inspite of high potentialities for industrial development and large scale public sector investment in industries, Bihar was at the bottom of industrial development in the country. United Bihar possessed 30 per cent of the value of minerals produced in India and yet Bihar remained one of the most ruralised regions of the country.

It was believed that whatever industrial development occurred in India before independence occurred as a result of the integration of the Indian economy with the world capitalist system through trade and capital investment. But on the contrary the major spurt in Indian industrial development took place precisely during those periods when India's colonial economic link with the world capitalist economy were temporarily weakened or disrupted. Even this limited industrial growth failed to take place in Bihar; on the other hand strengthening of these links led to backwardness and stagnation.

The regional matrix of growth in India calls for a separate analysis. The Eastern region had to face the main brunt of British capital and exploitation. Much as Bihar shares the fate of Eastern India generally, there are notable differences in the levels of industrialization in the Eastern sector itself. The economic backwardness of Bihar is not an isolated phenomenon. The underdevelopment of Bihar is the manifestation of a common, historically conditioned and structurally determined, development process that can be understood only with reference to the nature, structure and evaluation of the present national and international order. As we know, of all places Bengal Presidency (constituting Bengal, Bihar and Orissa) before independence was the original pasture of British colonialism in India.

The resources of the eastern India not only provided the fodder for the imperial war machine to conquer the rest of India but it also bridged the deficits of the presidencies of Bombay and Madras in the late 18th and early 19th centuries. This area witnessed systematic extermination of artisan and traders.

Against this background, we now discuss what had indeed prevented the emergence of regional entrepreneurial class in Bihar, which was earlier part of the Bengal Presidency. The answer to this query in terms of a poor material base of the local economy is undoubtedly appealing.

But we must also remember that there are parts of India, where material base has been equally poor and yet have seen the emergence of fairly buoyant regional entrepreneurs. This leads us to an enquiry into the possible link between regional identity and regional entrepreneurship which have been seen to emerge almost simultaneously in many parts of India. This phenomenon has been witnessed in the colonial period, as well as after independence.

As discussed above, the artisans and traders who could have been the main social base for provincial entrepreneurs faced widespread extermination during the early stages of colonial rule in the eastern region of India. The South and Western India felt the brunt of colonial rule at a very late stage, so the artisans and traders of this region survived the colonial depredations.

Secondly, Bihar being in the 'Permanent Settlement' area, the land tenurial system here was more iniquitous than in Ryotwari and Mahalwari areas.

Surplus generation and retention in the hands of the tenants of that surplus was least, as compared to the other tenurial systems. Thirdly, public investment during the British period created condition for strengthening the material base of the respective economy. Investment in canal and roads brought about dramatic changes in agricultural production and industrial development. Punjab, Western U.P., Coastal Region are testimony to the fact.

In Bihar, Sone Canal area which is the most developed agricultural track held this preeminent position even during the British period. Infact, Green Revolution was introduced in 1960's where there were captive water resources. It can be said with some amount of authority that no new area has developed in India, which was not developed in the pre-independence period. Since 1947, regional accumulation was dependent on devolution of resources by the Central government to the states.

On that count Bihar's record was very dismal. On the question of devolution of resources, either planned or non-planned, Bihar was always disadvantaged. The recent division of the State was the final blow, which has financially crippled the State.

To top this, there has not been any compensation from the Central government. In the realm of debt, Bihar is on the verge of financial trap.

Out of our Rs. 18,000 crore annual budget, we are not in a position to raise tax revenue of more than Rs. 3,000 crore. On the other hand, wo havc to pay Rs. 5,000 crore in the form of interest for our debt.

Non-Economic Constraints As noted earlier, nationalism first emerged as regional or sub-national phenomenon particularly in non-Hindi linguistic areas like Bengal, Gujarat, Maharashtra, etc. But in the Hindi Heartland, the regional phenomenon unfolded differently. Let us very briefly discuss about the problems of language and nationalities of this region.

## TRANSPORT

*Patna river port on national inland waterways-1 at Gai Ghat*

*Steamers and dredgers at Gai Ghat, Patna*

## Airways

Bihar has three operational airports: Lok Nayak Jayaprakash Airport, Patna; Gaya Airport; and Purnea Airport. The Patna airport is categorised as a restricted international airport, with customs facilities to receive international chartered flights. An airport at Muzaffarpur is under construction. Darbhanga Airport is scheduled to start operation in under UDAN 2 scheme.

## Inland Waterways

The Ganges – navigable throughout the year – was the principal river highway across the vast north Indo-Gangetic Plain. Vessels capable of accommodating five hundred merchants were known to ply this river in the ancient period; it served as a conduit for overseas trade, as goods were carried from Pataliputra (later Patna) and Champa (later Bhagalpur) out to the seas and to ports in Sri Lanka and Southeast Asia. The role of the Ganges as a channel for trade was enhanced by its natural links – it embraces all the major rivers and streams in both north and south Bihar.

# 7

# Tourism

## INTRODUCTION

*The Mahabodhi Temple, among the four holy sites related to the life of the Lord Buddha and UNESCO World Heritage Site*

The culture and heritage of Bihar can be observed from the large number of ancient monuments spread throughout the state. Bihar is visited by many tourists from around the world, with about 24,000,000 (24 million) tourists visiting the state each year.

In earlier days, tourism in the region was purely based on educational tourism, as Bihar was home of some prominent ancient universities like Nalanda & Vikramashila.

*Sabhyata Dwar in Patna*

*Monuments of Darbhanga*

*Remains of the ancient city of Vaishali*

*Trolley ride in Rajgir*

*The tomb of Sher Shah Suri is in the Sasaram town of Bihar*

*Barabar Caves – Asokan Inscription*

*Vikramshila Monastery*

*Buddha Smriti Park*

# TOURISM IN BIHAR

Bihar in eastern India is one of the oldest inhabited places in the world with a history going back 3000 years. The rich culture and heritage of Bihar is evident from the innumerable ancient monuments that are dotted all over the state. Bihar is home to many tourist attractions and is visited by large numbers of tourists from all over the world. Around total 6 million tourists visit Bihar every year.

## History of tourism

The documented history of tourism in Bihar region dates back to the 4th century BCE. Greek geographer Megasthenes (c. 350–290 BC)visited the region in reign of Chandragupta Maurya. His observations were recorded in *Indika*. Dionysius was son of Megasthenes, who visited Pataliputra in reign of Ashoka. Hsuan-Tsang and I Ching visited Nalanda to study in the 7th century. educational tourismas Bihar was home of some prominent ancient universities like Nalanda and Vikramashila.

## Archaeological sites

### *Excavation*

- Kumhrar
- Agam Kuan
- Barabar Caves
- Nalanda
- Vikramashila
- Kesaria

### *Ancient*

- Vishnupada Temple
- Mahabodhi Temple
- Sasaram
- Maner Sharif

- Pataliputra
- Brahmayoni Hill
- Pretshila Hill
- Ramshila Hill
- Thawe Mandir

***Forts***

- Rohtas Fort
- Sasaram Fort
- Palamu Fort
- Maner Fort
- Jalalgarh Fort
- Raj Mahal
- Munger Fort
- Hathua Fort
- Darbhanga Fort

***Pilgrimages***

Bihar one of the most sacred place of various religions like Hinduism, Buddhism, Jainism, Sikhism & Islam, Many tourist travel to Bihar to visit their pilgrimage.

Mahabodhi Temple, a Buddhist shrine and UNESCO World Heritage Site, is also situated in Bihar. Mahatma Gandhi Setu, Patna, is one of the longest bridge in the world.

***Hindu pilgrimages***

- Mahavir Mandir
- Sitamarhi
- Madhubani
- Punausa
- Buxar
- West Champaran
- Munger
- Jamui

- Maa Tara chandi Temple
- Sasaram
- Darbhanga
- Anga area
- Mithila region
- Patna
- Gaya
- Aurangabad
- Bhabua
- Thawe mandir
- indradamaneshwar mahadev mandir , Balgudar , Lakhisarai

***Sikh pilgrimages***

The capital of Bihar, Patna is one of the holiest city in Sikhism, as The tenth Guru of the Sikhs Guru Gobind Singh was born here in 1666 and spent his early years before moving to Anandpur.

Patna was also honoured by visits from Guru Nanak in 1509 as well as Guru Tegh Bahadur in 1666.

- Takht Shri Harmandir Saheb - is, one of the Five Takhts of the Sikhism. The Gurdwara at Patna Sahib is in remembrance of the birthplace of Guru Gobind Singh, The tenth Guru of the Sikhs.
- Gurdwara Pahila Bara - commonly known as Gurdwara Ghai Ghat, is dedicated to Guru Nanak Dev, who during his visit in to Patna stayed here in 1509 and later by Guru Tegh Bahadur along with his family visited this place in 1666.
- Gurdwara Gobind Ghat - is where the child Guru Gobind Singh used to play with his playmates on the bank of the Ganges. It is situated on the bank of river Ganges and hardly 200 yards from Takht Shri Harmandir Saheb. It is also known as Gurdwara Kangan Ghat.

- Gurdwara Guru ka Bagh - This Gurdwara is situated 2 miles far from the birthplace of Guru Gobind Singh.
- Gurdwara Bal Leela - This place is just few meters away from Takhat Patna Sahib. Guru ji were playing with other children during his childhoodied Gurdwara Bal Leela is also known as Maini Sangat.
- Gurdwara Handi Sahib - This Gurdwara was built in the memory of Guru Teg Bahadur. As Guru Tog Bahadur with Mata Gujri and Bala Preetam stayed here in 1728
- Gurdwara Taksali Sangat
- Gurdwara Chacha Phaggu Mal
- Gurdwara Pakki Sangat
- Gurdwara Bari Sangat Sri Guru Tegh Bahadur Ji Chauki.
- Rajplace Rajnagar madhubani

***Buddhism pilgrimages***

- Mahabodhi Temple, Bodh Gaya
- Vaishali
- Nalanda
- Rajgir
- Kesariya
- Vikramashila
- Areraj
- Pataliputra

***Islamic pilgrimages***

- Sasaram
- Maner Sharif
- Bihar Sharif
- Phulwari Sharif
- Gaya
- Aurangabad
- Siwan
- Katihar

- Bhagalpur
- Darbhanga
- Purnia

***Jain pilgrimages***

- Rajgir - Rajgir is supposed to be the birthplace of Munisuvrata, the twentieth Tirthankara
- Pawapuri - Bhagwan Mahavira, the last Jain Tirthankar, attained Nirvana from Pawapuri.
- Pataliputra
- Arrah
- Vikramashila
- Vaishali
- Champapur - Champapur is a Jain Teerth Kshetra. It is the place where all the five kalyanaks of Bhagwan Vasupujya have taken place. The tallest statue of Bhagwan Vasupujya which stands 31 Feet in height was built in Champapur in 2014. The Panch Kalyanak Pratishtha Mahotsav of the statue was done from 27 Feb to 3 Mar 2014.

***Other pilgrimages***

- Padri Ki Haveli
- Hawa Mahal

***Buildings and structures***

- Golghar
- Bihar Museum
- Patna Museum
- Sabhyata Dwar
- Kargil Chowk
- Mahatma Gandhi Setu
- Samrat Ashok International Convention Centre

## Museums

### *History museums*

- Bihar Museum - currently opened only partially and under construction, would be the state museum replacing Patna Museum.
- Patna Museum - is the state museum of Bihar. It was built by the British during the British Raj in the year 1917 to house the historical artefacts found in the vicinity of Patna.
- Jalan Museum
- Darbhanga Museum
- Nalanda Museum
- Bodh Gaya Museum
- Vaishali Museum
- Vikramshila Museum

### *Science museums*

- Patna Planetarium - is one of the largest planetariums in Asia. The Patna Planetarium was dedicated to the Nation and opened for the public from April 1, 1993.
- Srikrishna Science Centre - This institution forms a unit of the National Council of Science Museums, an autonoums body under the ministry of Culture. It is located at south-western corner of the Gandhi Maidan.

### *Eco Center*

- Valmiki National Park
- Vikramshila Gangetic Dolphin Sanctuary
- Kanwar Lake Bird Sanctuary
- Bhimbandh Wildlife Sanctuary
- Manjhar kund
- Dhuan Kund
- Sanjay Gandhi Jaivik Udyan - is classified as one of the 16 large zoos in the country and is also known as Patna Zoo. This is situated on Bailey Road in Patna.

- Kakolat Waterfall
- Telhar Waterfall
- Karkat Waterfall

***Fairs and festivals***

- Sonepur Fair
- Rajgir Mahotsav
- Patna Film Festival
- Chhath
- Sama Chakeva
- Pitrapaksh Fair

## IMPORTANT TOURISM PLACES–AGAM KUAN

Agam Kuan, literally "the unfathomable well" is said to date back to the period of Maurya emperor Ashoka, the great. It is located to the east of Patna, Bihar state, India.

The well is 4.5 meters in diameter and is well framed from outside. There are many legends associated with the well, the most ghastly one being that Ashoka beheaded his ninety-nine brothers and consigned their heads into this well before he proclaimed himself the emperor.

## Alamnagar Block

Alamnagar block is one of the administrative divisions of Madhepura district, Bihar state, India. The block has a population (2001 census) of 129,263. The block headquarters are located at a distance of 58 km from the district headquarters, namely, Madhepura. Agam Kuan, literally "the unfathomable well" is said to date back to the period of Maurya emperor Ashoka, the great. It is located to the east of Patna, Bihar state, India.

## Alpura

Alpura is a small village situated in the Madhubani district of Bihar.

## Araria

Araria is a city and a municipality in Araria district in the state of Bihar, India.

***Geography:*** Araria is located at 26.15° N 87.52° E. It has an average elevation of 47 metres (154 feet).

***Demographics:*** As of 2001 India census[GRIndia], Araria had a population of 60,594. Males constitute 54% of the population and females 46%.

Araria has an average literacy rate of 50%, lower than the national average of 59.5%; with 62% of the males and 38% of females literate. 18% of the population is under 6 years of age.

## AURANGABAD

Aurangabad district is one of the thirty-seven districts of Bihar state, India, and Aurangabad town is the administrative headquarters of this district. Aurangabad district is a part of Magadha division.

***Headquarters***: Aurangabad

***Area:*** 3,305 km?

***Population:*** Total: 1,539,988

***Rural:*** 1,421,936

***Urban:*** 118,052

***Sub Divisions:*** Aurangabad, Daud Nagar

***Blocks:*** Madanpur, Kutumbba, Daudnagar, Aurangabad, Barun, Obra, Dev, Nabinagar, Haspura, Goh, Rafiganj

***Agriculture:*** Paddy, Wheat, Lentils

***Industry:*** Carpet and Blanket Weaving

***Rivers:*** Son, Punpun, Auranga, Bataane, Morhar, Aadi

Aurangabad features in traditional records. The Saint Chyawan spent his life in this district, and gives his name to a product of the area, called Chyawanprash. According to Hindu mythology, a deity named a small town in the area Surya Devta. In modern times, the town's name is Deo, and is the location of a popular religious festival called Chhat puja.

## Aurangabad

Aurangabad is a city and a municipality in Aurangabad district in the state of Bihar, India. Aurangabad (pop. 118,052) is the district headquarters of the eponymous district. It is situated on the Grand Trunk Road. The people of this region primarily speak Bhojpuri, though there are also sizeable Magadhi speakers.

***History:*** The Magadha region was one of the oldest and strongest empires of the world in the Ancient period and its boundaries (600-250 BC) spread across to parts of the (now present) countries of Burma, Pakistan, Indonesia, Sri Lanka & Bangladesh, apart from India. This was the region about Megasthenes (3rd Century BC), a Greek writer, traveller and scholar wrote with much awe and inspiration about his empire and the people.

***Geography:*** Aurangabad is located at 24.75° N 84.37° E. It has an average elevation of 108 metres (354 feet).

***Demographics:*** As of 2001 India census[GRIndia], Aurangabad had a population of 79,351. Males constitute 53% of the population and females 47%. Aurangabad has an average literacy rate of 70%, higher than the national average of 59.5%; with 58% of the males and 42% of females literate. 15% of the population is under 6 years of age.

## Bagaha

Bagaha is a city and a municipality in Pashchim Champaran district in the state of Bihar, India.

***Geography:*** Bagaha is located at 24.53° N 85.03° E. It has an average elevation of 135 metres (442 feet).

***Demographics:*** As of 2001 India census[GRIndia], Bagaha had a population of 91,383. Males constitute 53% of the population and females 47%. Bagaha has an average literacy rate of 38%, lower than the national average of 59.5%; with 66% of the males and 34% of females literate. 19% of the population is under 6 years of age.

## Bahadurganj

Bahadurganj is a city and a notified area in Kishanganj district in the state of Bihar, India.

***Geography:*** Bahadurganj is located at 26.27° N 87.82° E. It has an average elevation of 51 metres (167 feet).

***Demographics:*** As of 2001 India census[GRIndia], Bahadurganj had a population of 28,224. Males constitute 53% of the population and females 47%. Bahadurganj has an average literacy rate of 34%, lower than the national average of 59.5%; with 69% of the males and 31% of females literate. 21% of the population is under 6 years of age.

## Bairgania

Bairgania is a city and a notified area in Sitamarhi district in the state of Bihar, India.

***Demographics:*** As of 2001 India census[GRIndia], Bairgania had a population of 34,821. Males constitute 53% of the population and females 47%. Bairgania has an average literacy rate of 43%, lower than the national average of 59.5%; with 66% of the males and 34% of females literate. 20% of the population is under 6 years of age.

## Bakhtiarpur

Bakhtiarpur is a city and a notified area in Patna district in the state of Bihar, India.

***Demographics:*** As of 2001 India census[GRIndia], Bakhtiarpur had a population of 32,288. Males constitute 53% of the population and females 47%. Bakhtiarpur has an average literacy rate of 53%, lower than the national average of 59.5%; with 63% of the males and 37% of females literate. 18% of the population is under 6 years of age.

## Bamra

Bamra, covering an area of 5149 sq. km, was one of the Princely states of India during the period of the British Raj, and was acceded to India on 1 January 1948.

The legend states that the first Raja of Bamra belonged to the ruling family of Patna. He is believed to have been stolen as a child and was made the ruler of the state of Bamra around 1602.

Most of the country is forest, producing only timber and lac but said to be rich in iron ore. The northern border is touched by the Bengal-Nagpur railway, with a station at Bamra town. The state is one of the five Uriya feudatories, which were transferred from the Central Provinces to Bengal, on the reconstitution of that province in October 1905. The capital is Deogarh.

## Rajas

| | | |
|---|---|---|
| 1865 | 1869 | Tribhuban Singh |
| 1869 | 1903 | Basu Deb Sudhal Deb |
| 1903 | 1916 | Satchitananda Tribhuban Deb |
| 1916 | 1920 | Dibyashankar Sudhal Deb |
| 1920 | 1947 | Bhanugang Tribhuban Deb |

## ARARIA

Araria district is one of the districts of Bihar state, India, and Araria town is the administrative headquarters of this district. Araria district is a part of Purnia division.

***Headquarters:*** Araria

***Area:*** 2,830 km?

***Population:*** Total: 1611638

***Rural:*** 1509360

***Urban:*** 102278

***Sub Divisions:*** Araria Farbisganj (also spelled Forbesganj)

***Blocks:*** Araria, Raniganj, Bharganwan, Kursakata, Sikti, Narpatganj, Farbisganj (also spelled Forbesganj), Palasi, Jokihat

***Agriculture:*** Paddy, Maize, Jute

***Industry:*** Jute Mills

***Rivers:*** Kosi, Suwara, Kali and Koli

Araria as a district was formed in January 1990 as one of the administrative districts of under Purnia Division. During the British period, the area where one Mr. Forbes's Bungalow was located was called "Residential Area", which people called as R. Area. Over a period of time, R. Area acquired the pronunciation *Arariya.* Renu ji (Phanishwar Nath 'Renu', legendary novelist and story writer, belonged to Ararai.

## Areraj

Areraj is a city and a notified area in Purba Champaran district in the state of Bihar, India.

***Demographics;*** As of 2001 India census[GRIndia], Areraj had a population of 20,245. Males constitute 52% of the population and females 48%. Areraj has an average literacy rate of 45%, lower than the national average of 59.5%; with 64% of the males and 36% of females literate. 20% of the population is under 6 years of age.

## Arrah

Arrah is a city and a municipality in Bhojpur district in the state of Bihar, India. It is the district headquarters of Bhojpur district and is located 36 miles from Patna.

***History;*** Arrah is an old city with references in mythological stories. It has been centre of attraction for Jainism with dozens of old temples and hermitages. Recently, it is known for a battle (Battle of Buxar) during the British occupation of India. During the Indian rebellion of 1857, a small party of British officers and Indian soldiers were besieged in the *Little House at Arrah*, the district headquarters. They withstood the siege for three weeks until relieved by British troops.

***Demographics:*** As of 2001 India census[GRIndia], Arrah had a population of 203,395. Males constitute 54% of the population and females 46%.

Arrah has an average literacy rate of 67%, higher than the national average of 59.5%; with 60% of the males and 40% of females literate.

## ARWAL

Arwal district is one of the thirty-seven districts of Bihar state, India, and Arwal town is the administrative headquarters of this district. Arwal district is a part of Magadha division.

***Headquarters:*** Arwal came into existence September 2001. It was earlier part of Jehanabad.

***Population:*** *Total:* 587229

***Blocks:*** Suryapur Banshi, Arwal, Kaler, Karpi, Kurtha

***Agriculture:*** Paddy, Wheat, Maize : Son

***River:*** Punpun

***Famous Company:*** Aups Multimedia (Mumbai). The owners of this company are from Arwal District. AUPS MULTIMEDIA is the most prestigious multimedia film company of India.

### Asarganj

Asarganj is a census town in Munger district in the state of Bihar, India.

***Geography:*** Asarganj is located at 25.15° N 86.68° E. It has an average elevation of 44 metres (144 feet).

***Demographics:*** As of 2001 India census[GRIndia], Asarganj had a population of 5706. Males constitute 53% of the population and females 47%.

Asarganj has an average literacy rate of 70%, higher than the national average of 59.5%; with 58% of the males and 42% of females literate. 14% of the population is under 6 years of age.

## BHOJPUR

Bhojpur (25°352 N 84°82 E) is an administrative district in the state of Bihar in India. The district headquarters are located at Arrah also known as Ara. The district occupies an area of 2,474 km² and has a population of 1,792,771 (as of 2001).

Bhojpur district is one of the thirty-eight districts of Bihar state, India, and Arrah town is the administrative headquarters of this district. Bhojpur district is a part of Patna division.

This area is known for its rich language—Bhojpuri.

This district played a major role in India's struggle for independence. Raja Shahrukh Khan of Jagdishpur was the leader of the mutineers during the first war of independence in 1857, called the sepoy mutiny by the British. The fighting was so severe that two of the five Victoria Crosses ever awarded to civilians by the British were awarded during this battle. A third VC was awarded to an army officer.

***Population:*** Total: 1,792,771

***Rural:*** 1,557,287

***Urban:*** 235,484

***Sub Divisions:*** Ara Sadar, Jagdishpur, Piro

***Blocks:*** Ara Sadar, Udwantnagar, Jagdishpur, Koilwar, Sahar, Barhara, Sandesh, Shahpur, Charpokhari, Piro, Tarari, Bihia, Agiawon, Garhani

***Agriculture:*** Rich Paddy Fields, Wheat, Maize.

***Industry:*** Rice and Oil Mills.

***Rivers:*** Ganges, Sone.

***Hotel:*** Shivam rest House, Station Road, Ara, Park View Hotel, near ramna maidan.

***Some Villages:*** Dhamar, Sinha Ghat, Babhangawan, Milki, Shambhuganj, Amarpur, Duroundha, Dhobhan, Dhamawal, Bharauli.

***Colleges:*** Maharaja College, Jagjivan College, Jain College, Brahamrishi College School-hnk high school, hpd jain school

## Bihar-E-Sharif

Bihar-E-Sharif, also called Bihar Sharif, is a small town in Nalanda district, Bihar, India. It is headquarter of Nalanda district.

The neighbouring places of tourist interest are Rajgir, Pawapuri and Nalanda. The town is mostly agriculture economy although a Railway coach factory is being built in Harnout.

The town is well connected by railway to all the major cities e.g. Delhi (Shramjeevi Express, 2392) (Magadha Express, 2401), Patna (Many local and Express trains are available at regular interval), Calcutta, Kanpur, Lucknow, Allahabad, Varanasi etc. and new project as per announcing in paper Harnout Sugar Cane mill, Bihar Sharif Cement Factory etc. Politically this small town has given some famous politicians like George Fernades, Nitish Kumar and more.

## Bihariganj Block

Bihariganj block is one of the administrative divisions of Madhepura district, Bihar state, India. The block has a population (2001 census) of 101,662. The block headquarters are located at a distance of 41 km from the district headquarters, namely, Madhepura. Bikramganj is a city and a notified area in Rohtas district in the state of Bihar, India.

***Geography:*** Bikramganj is located at 25.2° N 84.25° E. It has an average elevation of 77 metres (252 feet).

***Demographics:*** As of 2001 India census[GRIndia], Bikramganj had a population of 38,391. Males constitute 53% of the population and females 47%. Bikramganj has an average literacy rate of 58%, lower than the national average of 59.5%; with male literacy of 67% and female literacy of 48%. 19% of the population is under 6 years of age.

## Birpur

Birpur is a city and a notified area in Supaul district in the state of Bihar, India. It is a small town on the Indo-Nepal border near the historic Kosi Barrage on the Kosi River.

***Geography:*** Birpur is located at 25.53 N 83.85 E. It has an average elevation of 54 metres (177 feet).

***Demographics:*** As of 2001 India census[GRIndia], Birpur had a population of 17,730. Males constitute 54% of the population and females 46%. Birpur has an average literacy rate of 56%, lower than the national average of 59.5%; with male literacy of 65% and female literacy of 46%. 15% of the population is under 6 years of age.

## Budhi Gandak

Budhi Gandak is an important river but the other river named the *Gandak* is a much bigger river originating from the Himalayas in Nepal. The Budhi Gandak originates From West Champaran near Ramnagar and Bagaha, passes through various districts of Bihar (East Champaran, Muzaffarpur, Samastipur, Khagaria) and flows into Ganges river near Khagaria/Manasi.

## Chakia

Chakia is a city and a notified area in Purba Champaran district in the state of Bihar, India. The associate post office is called Bara Chakia, Pin Code 845412. It is served by a broad gauge train, directly connecting it to Calcutta, Delhi and rest of the country.

It has a sugar cane mill, that is now defunct. The railway station is called CHAKIA, it is also the closest railway station to Kesaria Stupa, a Buddhist pilgrimage site.

***Geography:*** Chakia is located at 26.42° N 85.05° E. It has an average elevation of 52 metres (170 feet).

***Demographics:*** As of 2001 India census[GRIndia], Chakia had a population of 16,618. Males constitute 53% of the population and females 47%. Chakia has an average literacy rate of 51%, lower than the national average of 59.5%; with male literacy of 60% and female literacy of 40%. 18% of the population is under 6 years of age.

## Chanpatia

Chanpatia is a city and a notified area in Pashchim Champaran district in the state of Bihar, India.

***Demographics:*** As of 2001 India census[GRIndia], Chanpatia had a population of 22,029. Males constitute 52% of the population and females 48%. Chanpatia has an average literacy rate of 49%, lower than the national average of 59.5%; with male literacy of 58% and female literacy of 39%. 19% of the population is under 6 years of age.

## Chapra

Chapra is a city and a district in the state of Bihar, India.

***History:*** The city is home to Jai Prakash Narayan and Jaiprakash Narayan University has been opened in the name of this stalwart of Indian politics. Dr. Rajendra Prasad, first President of India , a renowned scholar and statesman was a native of undivided Saran (Chapra). Chapra was once part of a greater district called Saran. Later, the larger district was divided into three separate districts: Chapra, Siwan, and Gopalganj.

Some of the memorials in the city include Majhrool Haq and the Temple of Ambaji at Ambikasthan Peerbaba, Kot ke Devi and Temple of Dharamnath Ji. Laloo Prasad Yadav is a noted politician in the Chapra district.

It is also famous for its Bhojpuri heritage .The famous "Bhikhari Thakur" is a famous person from Chapra, and is often referred to as the Shakespeare of Bhojpuri. "Mahendra Misir" also a famous person in Bhojpuri Folk songs. He had specially invented the "Purvi" a style of Bhojpuri Folk song. He was the master in playing of several types of instruments.

It is well known for Asia's biggest cattle mela at Sonpur. Maharshi Dadhichi was also belongs to Chapra who had donated his bone to Gods for manufacturing of arms. Cottage of Dronacharya was also situated in Chapra. The fight of "Gaj (Elephant) and "Grah" Corcodial was made at Sonepur in Chapra also. At Chirand in Chapra ancient (primitive) bones were found and are placed in the Chapra Museum. It is famous for King Maurayadyaj who was ready to sacrifice his only son to Vaman Avatar Lord Vishnu.

***Geography:*** Chapra is located at 25.773460° N 84.727470° E. It has an average elevation of 36 metres (118 feet).

Located just above the Gaghara River's junction with the Ganges, its 1991 population was 136,877 people. Chapra is a road and rail hub, as well as a centre for trade in agricultural products.

***Demographics:*** As of 2001 India census[GRIndia], Chapra had a population of 178,835. Males constitute 54% of the population and females 46%. Chapra has an average literacy rate of 61%, higher than the national average of 59.5%; with male literacy of 72% and female literacy of 48%. 15% of the population is under 6 years of age. Chapra is the headquarters of Saran district in the state of Bihar, India.

It has a long history from the era of Lord Ram. It was here that Lord Rama had released Ahilya from her stone statue status (due to the curse of her husband Gautam muni). Ramayana describes it as Ahilya-Uddhaar. This place is named as Gautam Sthan. Chapra is also the place where according to mythology when lord Shiva carried the dead body of Parvati from the holy yagnakund of Daksh Prajapati, the neck of Parvati's body fell and the holy Shaktipeeth Ambika Sthan was established.

This place is known today as Ambika sthan. Shivpuran has the details about the same. Mahadani King Mayurdvajh's palace's archeological remains are still found here, just on the bank of Ganga-Saryu sangam at Chirand area. Chapra also has maharshi Dadhichi's asharam. (Dadhichi was a great tapasawi, he has donated his bones to make Lord Indra's vajra to help them in fighting with asurs) After Independence, the first president of India Dr. Rajendra Prasad belonged to Chapra district.

Shri jayprakash narayan, Majharul Haq, Mahapandit Rahul Sankrityayan, Pandit Ramavatar Sharma, Pandit Kapil Dev Sharma and Bharat Mishra all belonged to the soil of Chapra. This place had also given 6 chief ministers to Bihar State. Chapra is a place to visit due to its many importances, it is as relevant today as it was in the past. The approach to the town is much easy through Train or Road.

The state capital Patna is only 70 km from here. The main language here is bhojpuri .Important educational institutions here are Rajendra college, Jagdam college and some small inter colleges.

In schools, Zila School, Visveswar Seminary, Saran Academy, Rajput School, Brahmin School are very good schools for boys whereas Govt. Girls' High School, Janak Yadav Girls High School, Arya Kanya Girls School et. are good schools for Girls. Apart from the govt. schools there are many private schools like Braj Kishore Kinder Garten, V. D. Academy, Saran Academy etc.

Therefore Chapra has a very good infrastructure for education. It is quite peaceful place as compare to its nearby places. Its main commercial places is Municipal chowk, this place is in the middle of town, therefore this is called heart of town. For shopping of cloths hathwa market is famous. On August 11, 2006 Union Rail Minister Laloo Yadav announced setting up of locomotive manufacturing unit in the district.

In festivals, besides Holi, Diwali and Id, there is Chhath Parv in which Sun is reshipped.

## Chousa Block

Chousa block is one of the administrative divisions of Madhepura district, Bihar state, India. The block has a population (2001 census) of 116,486. The block headquarters are located at a distance of 55 km from the district headquarters, namely, Madhepura.

## Colgong

Colgong is a city and a municipality in Bhagalpur district in the state of Bihar, India.

***Geography:*** Colgong is located at 25.27° N 87.22° E. It has an average elevation of 16 metres (52 feet).

***Demographics:*** As of 2001 India census[GRIndia], Colgong had a population of 22,110. Males constitute 53% of the population and females 47%. Colgong has an average literacy rate of 57%, lower than the national average of 59.5%: male literacy is 63% and, female literacy is 50%. In Colgong, 17% of the population is under 6 years of age.

## Dalsinghsarai

Dalsinghsarai is a city and a notified area in Samastipur district in the state of Bihar, India.

***Demographics:*** As of 2001 India census[GRIndia], Dalsinghsarai had a population of 20,181. Males constitute 53% of the population and females 47%. Dalsinghsarai has an average literacy rate of 60%, higher than the national average of 59.5%: male literacy is 69% and, female literacy is 51%. In Dalsinghsarai, 16% of the population is under 6 years of age.

## Danapur

Danapur is a satellite town of Patna in Bihar province of India on the right bank of the Ganges. In 1857 the sepoy garrison of the place initiated the rebellion of that year in Patna district, but after a conflict with the European troops were forced to retire from the town, and subsequently laid siege to Arrah. Basically, it is the Headquarter of Bihar Regiment of Indian Army. Danapur is also a Division of Eastern Central Zone of Indian Railway. The Divisional Railway Manager's (DRM) office is situated near Danapur Railway station.

The area surrounding to this station is called Khagaul. The Danapur Cantt and Danapur City is 5 kilometers away. There is also a Degree College, namely Bindeswari Singh College, affiliated with Magadha University, Bodh-Gaya .

Danapur is the Cantonment town adjacent to Patna in Bihar. Its one of the oldest European cantonments in the region. It was the only white cantonment of the East India Company between... It was the largest military cantonment in Bengal, with accommodation for two batteries of ARTILLERY European and a native infantry regiment. In 1857 the sepoy garrison of the place initiated the rebellion of that year in Patna district, but after a conflict with the European troops were forced to retire from the town, and subsequently laid siege to Arrah.

## DARBHANGA

Darbhanga District is one of the thirty-seven districts of

Bihar state, India, and Darbhanga town is the administrative headquarters of this district. Darbhanga district is a part of Darbhanga Division. The district comprises three civil Sub-divisions, 18 Blocks, 329 Panchayats, 1269 villages & 23 Police Stations.

***Area:*** 2,279 km?

***Population:*** Total: 25,10,959

***Rural:*** 22,92,568

***Urban:*** 2,18,391

***Sub Divisions:*** Darbhanga Sadar, Benipur, Biraul

***Blocks:*** Bahadurpur, Jale, Hayaghat, Singhwara, Benipur, Ghanshyampur, Baheri, Kewati, Manigachhi, Darbhanga, Biraul, Kusheswarsthan, Alinagar, Kusheswarsthan East, Gaura Vauram, Kiratpur, Hanuman Nagar, Tardih.

***Agriculture:*** Paddy

***Industry:*** Paper Mill, Sugar Factories, Handloom

***Rivers:*** Kamla, Balan, Bagmati.

Medical Facilities (Private) Rb Memorial Hospital, Jyoti Esearch Hospital, Life Care Hospital, Sisu Seba Sadan, Sharma Diagnostics, Charitable Hospital

## Universities

- *Lalit Narayan Mithila University:* L.N.M.university was established on 7 August, 1972, Darbhanga by dividing the Bihar University (now Baba Saheb Bhim Rao Ambedkar University), Muzaffarpur. It was shifted in the building of Darbhanga Raj in 1975.
- *Kameshwarsingh Sanskrit University:* Sanskrit University building was established in 1961. A great learned Mahamhopadhyay Dr. Umesh Mishra was the first Vice Chancellor of this University. Nearly 5500 rare manuscripts on Epic, Philosophy, Vyakaran, Dharmashastra, etc. the few manuscripts of Vidyapati, Mahesh Thakur in there own scripts are preserved in the University. The post Graduate Department is corporated

with the Veda, the Vyakarna, the Dharma Shastra, the Darshana, the Jyotish & the Sahitya are functioning.

***Darbhanga Division:*** Darbhanga Division is an administrative geographical unit of Bihar state of India, and Darbhanga town is the administrative headquarters of the division. As of 2005, the division consists of Darbhanga District, Madhubani District, Samastipur District, and Begusarai District.

## Daudnagar

Daudnagar is a city and a municipality in Aurangabad district in the state of Bihar, India.

***Geography:*** Daudnagar is located at 25.03° N 84.4° E. It has an average elevation of 84 metres (275 feet).

***Demographics:*** As of 2001 India census[GRIndia], Daudnagar had a population of 37,977. Males constitute 52% of the population and females 48%. Daudnagar has an average literacy rate of 55%, lower than the national average of 59.5%: male literacy is 63% and, female literacy is 46%. In Daudnagar, 18% of the population is under 6 years of age.

## Dehri

Dehri is a city and a municipality in Rohtas district in the state of Bihar, India.

***Geography:*** Dehri is located at 24.87° N 84.18° E. It has an average elevation of 99 metres (324 feet).

***Demographics:*** As of 2001 India census[GRIndia], Dehri had a population of 119,007. Males constitute 53% of the population and females 47%. Dehri has an average literacy rate of 66%, higher than the national average of 59.5%: male literacy is 74% and, female literacy is 57%. In Dehri, 15% of the population is under 6 years of age.

## Dighwara

Dighwara is a city and a notified area in Saran district in the state of Bihar, India. Name probably emerged from 'Dirghdwar' or literally 'lagre gate'. This place is said to be the entrance gate of the mythological city of king Daksha. The town is on the banks of ganga.

***Geography:*** Dighwara is located at 25.73° N 85.0° E. It has an average elevation of 43 metres (141 feet).

***Demographics:*** As of 2001 India census[GRIndia], Dighwara had a population of 27,327. Males constitute 52% of the population and females 48%. Dighwara has an average literacy rate of 48%, lower than the national average of 59.5%: male literacy is 59% and, female literacy is 35%. In Dighwara, 19% of the population is under 6 years of age.

## BANKA

Banka is an administrative district in the state of Bihar in India, with district headquarters at Banka town. The district occupies an area of 3018 km$^2$ and has a population of 1,608,778 (as of 2001).

Banka district is a part of Bhagalpur Division.

***Population:*** Total: 150113

***Rural:*** 145560

***Urban:*** 4553

***Sub Divisions:*** Banka

***Blocks:*** Banka, Rajon, Amarpur, Dhoraiya, Katoria, Bausi, Shambhuganj, Barahat, Belhar, Chandan, Phulidumar

***Agriculture:*** Paddy, Wheat, Maize, Lentil

Banka is a city and a municipality in Banka district in the state of Bihar, India.

***Geography:*** Banka is located at 24.88° N 86.92° E. It has an average elevation of 79 metres (259 feet).

***Demographics:*** As of 2001 India census[GRIndia], Banka had a population of 35,416. Males constitute 54% of the population and females 46%. Banka has an average literacy rate of 55%, lower than the national average of 59.5%; with 61% of the males and 39% of females literate. 16% of the population is under 6 years of age.

## Bankipur

Bankipur is a residential area in Patna in the Indian state of Bihar. It is located on the bank of the river Ganges. The prime attraction is Golghar that was built by Captain John Garstir in 1786. Patna Dental College and Hospital is also located here. It is believed that E. M. Forster based the city of Chandrapore in his novel *A Passage to India* on this town.

## Banmankhi Bazar

Banmankhi Bazar is a city and a notified area in Purnia district in the state of Bihar, India.

***Demographics:*** As of 2001 India census[GRIndia], Banmankhi Bazar had a population of 25,183. Males constitute 55% of the population and females 45%. Banmankhi Bazar has an average literacy rate of 52%, lower than the national average of 59.5%; with 64% of the males and 36% of females literate. 18% of the population is under 6 years of age.

## Barahiya

Barahiya is a city and a municipality in Lakhisarai district in the state of Bihar, India.

***Demographics:*** As of 2001 India census[GRIndia], Barahiya had a population of 39,745. Males constitute 53% of the population and females 47%. Barahiya has an average literacy rate of 59%, below than the national average of 59.9%; with 61% of the males and 39% of females literate. 15% of the population is under 6 years of age.

## Barauli

Barauli is a city and a notified area in Gopalganj district in the state of Bihar, India.

***Geography:*** Barauli is located at 26.4° N 84.58° E. It has an average elevation of 65 metres (213 feet).

***Demographics:*** As of 2001 India census[GRIndia], Barauli had a population of 34,643. Males constitute 49% of the population and females 51%. Barauli has an average literacy rate of 41%, lower than the national average of 59.5%; with 64% of the males and 36% of females literate. 20% of the population is under 6 years of age.

## Barauni

Barauni is a town in the state of Bihar, India.

***Barauni IOC Township:*** Barauni IOC Township is a census town in Begusarai district in the state of Bihar, India.

***Demographics:*** As of 2001 India census[GRIndia], Barauni IOC Township had a population of 13,825. Males constitute 55% of the population and females 45%. Barauni IOC Township has an average literacy rate of 77%, higher than the national average of 59.5%; with 58% of the males and 42% of females literate. 13% of the population is under 6 years of age.

## Barbigha

Barbigha is a city and a notified area in Sheikhpura district in the state of Bihar, India.

***Demographics:*** As of 2001 India census[GRIndia], Barbigha had a population of 38,258. Males constitute 53% of the population and females 47%. Barbigha has an average literacy rate of 52%, lower than the national average of 59.5%; with 63% of the males and 37% of females literate. 19% of the population is under 6 years of age.

## Barh

Barh is a city and a municipality in Patna district in the state of Bihar, India. It is located on the Ganges River, 34 miles southeast of Patna.

***Geography:*** Barh is located at 25.48° N 85.72° E. It has an average elevation of 47 metres (154 feet).

***Demographics;*** As of 2001 India census[GRIndia], Barh had a population of 48,405. Males constitute 54% of the population and females 46%.

Barh has an average literacy rate of 59%, lower than the national average of 59.5%; with 60% of the males and 40% of females literate. 15% of the population is under 6 years of age.

## Fatuha Block

Fatuha (also Fatwah) is one of the 20 blocks of Barh. It is about 25 kilometres east of Patna, lying on the banks of the Ganges River and is the confluence of the Punpun river and Ganges. Its well connected by trains on Howrah- Delhi main line, falling under the Danapur East central railway division of the Indian railways.

The Grand-Trunk road connects Fatuha to the rest of the Bihar.

It had a scooter factory as well as a tractor factory. The sayings as per the locals goes that it was known as "PATWA" due to the large numbers of patwas or weavers living in here. The name gradually changed during the colonial rule as per their pronunciation.

The year of establishment was 2 October 1957. The total geographical area is 12016.45 hectares.

The Indian Railways station code is FUT. Subscriber Trunk Dialing code is 0612. The nearest airport is Lok Nayak Jayaprakash Airport.

## Begusarai

Begusarai is a city and a municipality in Begusarai district in the state of Bihar, India.

***Geography:*** Begusarai is located at 25.42° N 86.13° E. It has an average elevation of 41 metres (134 feet).

***Demographics:*** As of 2001 India census[GRIndia], Begusarai had a population of 93,378. Males constitute 53% of the population and females 47%. Begusarai has an average literacy rate of 65%, higher than the national average of 59.5%; with 59% of the males and 41% of females literate. 15% of the population is under 6 years of age.

## BEGUSARAI

Begusarai district is one of the thirty-seven districts of Bihar state, India, and Begusarai town is the administrative headquarters of this district. Begusarai district is a part of Darbhanga division. It was established in 1870 as a subdivision of Munger District. In 1972, it was given district status. The name of the district apparently comes from Begu, a man who looked after *Sarai*, an old and small inn.

It is represented in Parliament of India by Rajeev Ranjan Singh of the Janata Dal (United).

***Headquarters:*** Begusarai Location : latitudes 25.15N & 25.45N and longitudes 85.45E & 86.36E

***Area:*** 1918.0km?

***Population:*** Total: 2342989

***Sub Divisions:*** Begusarai, Manjhaul, Ballia, Bakhari, Teghara.

***Blocks:*** 18

***Agriculture:*** *Kharif*: Paddy, Arahar, Urad. *Rabi*: Wheat, Macca, Gram, Masur, Mater, Mustard, Tisi, Sunflower.

***Cash Corps :*** oilseeds, tobacco, jute, potato, red chilies, tomato and andi.

***Industry:*** Indian Oil Refinery- Barauni, Thermal power station- Barauni and hundreds of small industrial units in the private sector.

***Rivers:*** Ganga, Burhi Gandak, Balan, Bainty, Baya and Chandrabhaga.

***Kaver Jheel:*** Kaver Jheel one of the Asia's largest fresh water lake, also famous for Birds' sanctuary.

***Noteworthy :*** Bridge across Ganges at Barauni, Resting spot for migratory birds, Industrial complex at Barauni

### Behea

Behea is a small town and a notified area in Bhojpur district in the state of Bihar, India.

***Demographics;*** As of 2001 India census[GRIndia], Behea had a population of 20,809. Males constitute 53% of the population and females 47%. Behea has an average literacy rate of 59%, lower than the national average of 59.5%; with 59% of the males and 41% of females literate. 17% of the population is under 6 years of age.

This town is alternatively spelled as Bihiya. The town boasts of a railway station and is a business hub for small time traders, who mainly collect agricultural produce from the farmers and sell in larger cities and even in neighbouring countries. There are a handful of timber traders too, who get timber and stone slabs from bigger cities and supply it to the villagers, who use it for construction of their house.

Another reason why many people visit the town is because of the "Mahthin Mai" temple. Its considered to be very holy for Hindus and the temple compound hosts a number of fairs.

## Belsand

Belsand is a city and a notified area in Sitamarhi district in the state of Bihar, India.

***Geography:*** Belsand is located at 26.45° N 85.4° E. It has an average elevation of 55 metres (180 feet).

***Demographics:*** As of 2001 India census[GRIndia], Belsand had a population of 17,821. Males constitute 53% of the population and females 47%. Belsand has an average literacy rate of 33%, lower than the national average of 59.5%; with 66% of the males and 34% of females literate. 19% of the population is under 6 years of age.

## Bettiah

Bettiah is the headquarters of West Champaran district in the state of Bihar, near Indo-Nepal border, 225 Kilometres north-west of Patna. It is located at 26.81°N Latitude and 84.50°E Longitude, 65 metres above Mean Sea Level. Bettiah, pronounced as 'Betiya', derived its name from 'baint' (local name for 'cane'), which was grown here extensively in the past but not now. Its spelling - Bettiah was given by British and it remains so. The most accepted and widely used code for it BTH.

***History:*** Birthplace of famous writer Gopal Singh Nepali, Mohandas Gandhi started the Satyagraha movement from Bettiah in 1919. The region surrounding Bettiah was being extensively used for Indigo plantation.

Though Indigo cultivation yielded quick benefits to the British Colonizers, a few years of Indigo cultivation would render the subsoil entirely devoid of nutients thereby effectively ruining any further cultivation of any kind . To this date, the adjoining regions which were being used for Indigo cultivation are barren & have only scrub vegetation in stark contrast to the lush greens typical of the highly fertile Indo-Gangetic Plains in which the West Champaran district lies.

West Champaran District was carved out of the old Champaran District in the year 1972 as a result of re-organization of the District in the state. It was formerly a subdivision of Saran District and then Champaran District with its Head quarters as Bettiah. It is said that Bettiah got its name from Baint (Cane) plants commonly found in this district. The name Champaran is a degenerate form of Champaka aranya, a name which dates back to the time when the district was a tract of the forest of Champa (Magnolia) trees & was the abode of solitary asectics.

As per District Gazetteer, it seems probable that Champaran was occupied at an early period by races of Aryan descent and formed part of the country in which the Videha empire ruled. After the fall of Videhan empire the district formed part of the Vrijjain oligarchical republic with its capital at Vaishali of which Lichhavis were the most powerful and prominent. Ajatshatru the emperor of Magadha, by tact and force annexed Lichhavis and occupied its capital, Vaishali. He extended his sovereignty over Paschim Champaran which continued under the Mauryan rule for the next hundred years.

After the Mauryas, the Sungas and Kanvas ruled over the Magadha territories. The district thereafter formed part of the

Kushan empire and then came under Gupta empire. Along with Tirhut, Champaran was possibly annexed by Harsha during whose reign Huen- Tsang, the famous Chinese pilgrim, visited India. During 750 to 1155 AD , the Palas of Bengal were in the possession of Eastern India and Champaran formed the part of their territory. Towards the close of the 10th century Gangaya Deva of the Kalacheeri dynasty conquered Champaran . He was succeeded by Vikramaditya of the Chalukya dynasty.

During 1213 and 1227, the first Muslim influence was experienced when Ghyasuddin Iwaz the Muslim governor of Bengal extended his influence over Tribhukti or Tirhut . It was however, not a complete conquest and he was only able to have Tirhut from Narsinghdeva, a Simraon king.

In about 1320, Ghyasuddin Tughluq annexed Tirhut to the Tughluq Empire and placed it under Kameshwar Thakur, who established Sugaon or Thakur dynasty. This dynasty continued to rule the area till Nasrat Shah, son of Alauddin Shah attacked Tirhut in 1530, annexed the territory, and killed the Raja and thus put an end to the Thakur dynasty. Nasrat Shah appointed his son-in-law as viceroy of Tirhut and thence forward the country continued to be ruled by the Muslim rulers. After the fall of Mughal Empire the British rulers came to power in India.

The history of the district during the late medieval period and the British period is linked with the history of Bettiah Raj. Bettiah Raj has been mentioned as a great estate. It traces its descent from one Ujjain Singh and his son, Gaj Singh, who reccived the title of Raja from the Emperor Shah Jahan (1628-58). The family came into prominence as independent chief in the 18th century during the downfall of the Mughal Empire. At the time when Sarkar Champaran passed under British rule, is was in the possession of Raja Jugal Kishore Singh, who succeeded Raja Dhurup Singh in 1763.

The Raj was succeeded by the descendents of Raja Jugal Kishore Singh. Harendra Kishore Singh, the last Maharaja of Bettiah, died in 1893, issueless and was succeeded by his first wife, who died in 1896. The estate came under the management of Court of Wards since 1897 and was held by the Maharaja's junior widow, Maharani Janki Kuar.

The British Raj palace occupies a large area in the centre of the town. In 1910 at the request of Maharani, the palace was built after the plan of Graham's palace in Calcutta. The Court Of Wards is at present holding the property of Bettiah Raj.

## Bettiah

The rise of nationalism in Bettiah in early 20th century is intimately connected with indigo plantation. Raj Kumar Shukla, an ordinary raiyat and indigo cultivator of Champaran met Gandhijii and explained the plight of the cultivators and the atrocities of the planters on the raiyats. Gandhiji came to Champaran in 1917 and listened to the problems of the cultivators and the started the movement known as Champaran Saryagraha Movement to end the oppression of the British indigo planters. By 1918 the long standing misery of the indigo cultivators came to an end and Champaran became the hub of Indian National Freedom Movement and the launch pad of Gandhi's Satyagraha.

***Geography:*** Bettiah is located at 26.8° N 84.5° E. It has an average elevation of 65 metres (213 feet).

***Demographics:*** As of 2001 India census[GRIndia], Bettiah had a population of 116,692. Males constitute 53% of the population and females 47%. Bettiah has an average literacy rate of 65%, higher than the national average of 59.5%; with 58% of the males and 42% of females literate. 17% of the population is under 6 years of age.

## Bhabua

Bhabua is the headquarters of Kaimur district in the state of Bihar, in India. Ruiyan is a village in bhabua block. it is 9km north from Bhabua. Bhabua town is divided in wards. In west, there is a river called Suwara. Mundeshwari Mandir is situated on the hill is 12 km from Bhabua. It is a very good place to see the nature.

Bhabua Road is the nearest Railway Station on the Howrah-New Delhi Grand Card.

The main trains are Purushottam Exp, Mahabodhi Exp, Poorva Exp, Kalka Mail, Mumbai Mail, Doon Exp etc. The town is 195 km from Patna and 84 km from Varanasi by road. Mother Toungue of almost all the people in Bhabua is Bhojpuri.

***Schools:*** High School Bhabua, Atal Bihari Singh H/S Bhabua, Girls High school Bhabua College: S.V.P. Degree College, Bhabua.

## BHAGALPUR

Bhagalpur District is one of the thirty-seven districts of Bihar state, India, and Bhagalpur town is the administrative headquarters of this district. Bhagalpur district is a part of Bhagalpur Division.

***Headquarters:*** Bhagalpur

***Area:*** 2,570 $km^2$

***Population:*** Total: 1909967

***Rural:*** 1566518

***Urban:*** 343449

***Sub Divisions:*** Bhagalpur, Kahalgaon, Naugachhia

***Blocks:*** Pirpainti, Kahalgoan, Sanhaula, Sabour, Nathnagar, Jagdishpur, Sultanganj purushottam (thana road), Sahkund, Bihpur, Navgachia, Gopalpur, Kharik, Narayanpur, Gauradih, Ismailpur, Rangrachowk

***Agriculture:*** Paddy, Maize, Lentils

***Industry:*** Tusser Silk, Thermal Power at Kahalgaon

***Rivers:*** Ganga

***Bhagalpur Division:*** Bhagalpur division is an administrative geographical unit of Bihar state of India, with Bhagalpur as the administrative headquarters of the division. As of 2005, the division consists of Bhagalpur District, Banka District, and Navgachia District.

## SAHARSA

Saharsa District is one of the thirty-seven districts of Bihar state, India, and Saharsa town is the administrative headquarters of this district.

Saharsa district is a part of Kosi Division and it became a district on 1 April 1954 a subsequently has become smaller with other districts being carved form it, most notably Madhepura in 1981.

***Headquarters:*** Saharasa

***Area:*** 1,696 km?

***Population:*** Total: 1132413

***Rural:*** 1052264

***Urban:*** 80149

***Sub Divisions:*** Saharasa Sadar, Simri Bakhtiyarpur

***Blocks:*** Nauhatta, Simari, Bakhatiyarpur, Salkhua, Kahra, Mahishi, Sonbarsa, Saurbazar, Patarghat, Sattar, Kateya, Banma Itahari

***Agriculture:*** Paddy

***Industry:*** Jute Factory

***Rivers:*** Kosi, Baghmati,

***Villages:*** Teghra, Bangaon, Chainpur, Parari, Soha, Sonpura, Ghazipeta, Dumra, Garual, Mahisi, Patarghat, Panchgachhia

***College:*** MLT saharsa college, Sarva Narayan Singh college, R M College, Saharsa College

Saharsa has distinction of producing great scholars like Mandan Mishra who was engaged in the historical debate with Shankaracharya. The story goes that when Shankara was searching for Mandan Mishra's house he came across some women washing clothes. When he asked for directions to the house he was told :

*jagaddhruvam syajjagadadhruvam syatkirangana yatra giram giranti,* dwarasthanidantarasannirudha janihi tanmandanamishrasadmah.

"Is the world permanent or non-permanent? Where you find the female parrots in cages at the front door discussing this question, that you may know to be the house of Mandan Mishra."

It shows the scholarly atmosphere at the house of Mandan Mishra.

The place surrounded on the west by the river Kosi boasts an abundance of fish, milk, makhana. The great saint "shree shree 108 paramhans goswami laxminath" was born in parsharma (Saharsa). His big ashram is located in Bangaon.

## NALANDA

Nalanda District is one of the thirty-eight districts of Bihar state, India, and Bihar Sharif town is the administrative headquarters of this district. Nalanda district is a part of Patna Division.

***Headquarters:*** Bihar Sharif

***Area:*** 2,367 km?

***Population:*** Total: 1997995

***Rural:*** 1701777

***Urban:*** 296218

***Sub Divisions:*** Bihar Sharif, Rajgir, Hilsa

***Blocks:*** Giriyak, Rahui, Nursarai, Harnaut, Chandi, Islampur (Nalanda), Rajgir, Asthawan, Sarmera, Hilsa, Biharsharif, Ekangarsarai, Ben, Nagarnausa, Karaiparsurai, Silao, Parwalpur, Katrisarai, Bind, Tharthari

***Agriculture:*** Rich Paddy Fields, Potato, Onion.

***Industry:*** Handloom weaving

***Rivers:*** Phalgu, Mohane

***Villages:*** Bangpur

### Narkatiaganj

Narkatiaganj is a city and a notified area in Pashchim Champaran district in the Indian state of Bihar.

***Demographics:*** As of 2001 India censusGRIndia, Narkatiaganj had a population of 40,830. Males constitute 54% of the population and females 46%. Narkatiaganj has an average literacy rate of 59%, lower than the national average of 59.5%: male literacy is 68%, and female literacy is 49%. In Narkatiaganj, 17% of the population is under 6 years of age.

## GAYA

Gaya is a district of Bihar. [For detailed information on History, Geography, Transportation, Lifestyle, and other details visit Gaya, India]

***Headquarters:*** Gaya

***Area:*** 4,976 km?

***Population:*** Total: 2664803

***Rural:*** 2308908

***Urban:*** 355895

***Sub Divisions:*** Gaya Sadar, Neemchak, Bathani, Sherghati, Tekari

***Blocks:*** Atri,Belaganj, Mohanpur, Konch-block, Barachatti, Manpur, Gurua, Tekari, Imamganj, Gaya, Sadar, Wazirganj, Fatehpur, Paraiya, Sherghati, Bodh Gaya, Khizarsarai, Amas, Dumaria, Bankey Bazar, Dobhi, Tankuppa, Nimchakbathani, Guraru, Muhra

***Agriculture:*** Paddy, Wheat, Potato, Lentils

***Temperature:*** 02 degree C - 59 degree C

***Industry:*** Oil mills, Sugar factory, Lac

***Rivers:*** Falgu

## Ghailardh Block

Ghailardh block is one of the administrative divisions of Madhepura district, Bihar state, India. The block has a population (2001 census) of 72,701. The block headquarters are located at a distance of 32 km from the district headquarters, namely, Madhepura.

## Ghoghardiha

Ghoghardiha is a city and a notified area in Madhubani district in the state of Bihar, India.

***Demographics:*** As of 2001 India census[GRIndia], Ghoghardiha had a population of 14,523. Males constitute 51% of the population and females 49%. Ghoghardiha has an average literacy rate of 43%, lower than the national average of 59.5%: male literacy is 53%, and female literacy is 33%.

In Ghoghardiha, 18% of the population is under 6 years of age. This is second last railway station to Nirmali. This place has a meter gauge track and not much frequent travelling facility is available. The majority of the people are workers who depend on farming. Fish is the most acceptable food notwithstanding many more are vegetarian.

## Gogri Jamalpur

Gogri Jamalpur is a city and a notified area in Khagaria district in the Indian state of Bihar.

***Demographics:*** As of 2001 India census[GRIndia], Gogri Jamalpur had a population of 31,093. Males constitute 53% of the population and females 47%. Gogri Jamalpur has an average literacy rate of 48%, lower than the national average of 59.5%: male literacy is 56%, and female literacy is 39%. In Gogri Jamalpur, 20% of the population is under 6 years of age.

## Golghar

Golghar, is located to the west of the Gandhi Maidan in Patna, capital of Bihar state, India . Disturbed by the devastating famine of 1770, Captain John Garstin got this Silo or beehive shaped structure built for the purpose of storing grains for the British army. It has a storing capacity of 140000 tons and was completed on 20th July 1786. At that time, India was under the British Raj.

It has a foundation of 125m, and a height of 29m. It is pillarless with the wall of 3.6m width at the bottom. One can climb atop the Golghar through the 145 steps of its winding stairway around the monument. The top of the Golghar presents a wonderful panoramic view of the city and the Ganga flowing nearby.

## Gopalganj

Gopalganj is a city and a municipality in and the headquarter of Gopalganj district in the Indian state of Bihar.

***Geography:*** Gopalganj is located at 26.47° N 84.43° E. It has an average elevation of 66 metres (216 feet).

***Demographics:*** As of 2001 India census[GRIndia], Gopalganj had a population of 54,418. Males constitute 53% of the population and females 47%. Gopalganj has an average literacy rate of 63%, higher than the national average of 59.5%: male literacy is 70%, and female literacy is 55%. In Gopalganj, 15% of the population is under 6 years of age.

## Goraul

Goraul is a town in Vaishali district in the state of Bihar, India.

***Geography:*** Goraul is located at 25.92225° N 85.32397° E. It has an average elevation of 55 metres (141 feet). Earlier here used to be a Sugar Mill, but now it has shut down. This place has given a lot in information technology development. Goraul has a Railway Station that facilitates Indian Railway to grow. Goraul participates a major role in Bihar economical development with the following - (1) Mango garden (2) Leechee garden (3) Betel garden

## Demographics

***Politics:*** Goraul plays a mejor part in Bihar as well as in Indian politics.

## Gwalpara Block

Gwalpara block is one of the administrative divisions of Madhepura district, Bihar state, India. The block has a population (2001 census) of 95,138. The block headquarters are located at a distance of 23 km from the district headquarters, namely, Madhepura.

## Habibpur

Habibpur is a census town in Bhagalpur district in the Indian state of Bihar.

***Demographics:*** As of 2001 India census[GRIndia], Habibpur had a population of 9360. Males constitute 53% of the population and females 47%. Habibpur has an average literacy rate of 40%, lower than the national average of 59.5%: male literacy is 46%, and female literacy is 33%. In Habibpur, 20% of the population is under 6 years of age.

## Hajipur

The introduction to this article provides insufficient context for those unfamiliar with the subject matter. Please help improve the introduction to meet Wikipedia's layout standards.

You can discuss the issue on the talk page. Hajipur is the headquarters of Vaishali district in the state of Bihar, in India.

***Origin of Name:*** In ancient times after crossing the Ganges at Patna the first village one came to the other side was Ukkacala, now called Hajipur.

***History:*** Hajipur is also of interest because a portion of Ananda's ashes were enshrined in the town. Ananda acted as the Buddha's personal attendant for twenty years and outlived him by several decades.

## Hajipur

A Hindu temple on it situated in the western outskirts of Hajipur. Go to the centre of town and ask for the way to Ramchaura. The temple on the top of the stupa is called Ramchaura Mandir. A few years ago it was made the zonal office of East Central Railways.

***Around Hajipur:*** Vaishali, Sonepur.

***Location:*** Hajipur is 10 kilometres across the Ganges from Patna.

***Coordinates:*** Hajipur (Bihar)

X: 9490000m

Y: 2945000m

Lat: 25:42:45N (25.7126)

Lon: 85:15:00E (85.2501)

***Transport:*** Nearest Transport Links:

- Patna Airport—13.2 miles (21.2 km).
- Hajipur is well connected by rail and road.

***Rail Link:*** Hajipur is the headquarters of East Central Railways. Three rail lines connect it to Muzaffarpur, Sonepur and Barauni. Important trains like Guwahati Rajdhani and Vaishali Express have got stops here.

***Road Link:*** Buses and auto rickshaws connect the city with the state capital Patna. Buses are also available to Muzaffarpur and Chapra.

## Hilsa, Bihar

Hilsa is a city and a notified area in Nalanda district in the Indian state of Bihar.

***Geography:*** Hilsa is located at 25.32° N 85.28° E. It has an average elevation of 45 metres (147 feet).

***Demographics:*** As of 2001 India census[GRIndia], Hilsa had a population of 37,748. Males constitute 54% of the population and females 46%. Hilsa has an average literacy rate of 57%, lower than the national average of 59.5%: male literacy is 66%, and female literacy is 46%. In Hilsa, 17% of the population is under 6 years of age.

## Hisua

Hisua is a city and a notified area in Nawada district in the Indian state of Bihar.

Livelihood of most of the people is agriculture and this is one of the most backward area of the state of Bihar. Many labours from this region have migrated to Mauritius, Reunion Islands and Caribbean island during mid of last century (Around 1850 ) .

Zamindari Pratha was prevalent in Hisua till 1950 and most of the agricultural land in Hisua were under a local Zamindar named "Babu Madan Mohan Lal". With the abolition of Zamindari Pratha by Vinobha Bhave in 1953 the agricultural land was distributed to the local villagers but the after affect of Zaminadari Pratha and the caste system can still be seen in this village .

***Geography:*** Hisua is located at 24.83° N 85.42° E. It has an average elevation of 93 metres (305 feet).

***Demographics:*** As of 2001 India census[GRIndia], Hisua had a population of 25,045. Males constitute 52% of the population and females 48%. Hisua has an average literacy rate of 51%, lower than the national average of 59.5%: male literacy is 59%, and female literacy is 41%. In Hisua, 18% of the population is under 6 years of age.

***Language:*** Magahi is the most popular language of this town . Along with Magahi people speak Bhojpuri and Hindi.

***Comunities—Musahars:*** Musahars or Mush-Rat Hars-eaters is the majority community who resides in this village. "Mush" is a Hindi word which means Rats and "Har" means eaters in Hindi . They are mostly peasents which feed on rats along with the wheat and paddy they grow in their land.

***Chamars & Doms:*** Chamars and Doms are the second most popular community of this village . Chamar are basically a leather craftsman which makes leather shoes and leather bags after extracting the leather from the dead domestic stocks . Doms are the scvanger community which clean the human and animal feces. Mention of these three communities can also be found in many of the stories and nobella of famous Hindi writer Premchand.

The above three communities are still considered untouchables even after 59 years of Indian Independence .

***Famous Sweet:*** Hisua is also famous for a sweet named "Tilkut". Its a very popular sweet in the entire Magadha region.

***Indrapuri Barrage:*** Indrapuri Dam is one of the longest dams in India, built on the Son River, storing a large amount of water. It is located nearly 5 km from Dehri. From it flow 2 major and several other small canals which supply the whole of western and central Bihar with water for irrigation.

## Islampur (Nalanda)

Please see disambiguation page Islampur Islampur is a city and a notified area in Nalanda district in the Indian state of Bihar.

***Geography:*** Islampur is located at 25.15° N 85.2° E.dilip It has an average elevation of 63 metres (206 feet).

***Demographics:*** As of 2001 India census[GRIndia], Islampur had a population of 29,855. Males constitute 53% of the population and females 47%. Islampur has an average literacy rate of 54%, lower than the national average of 59.5%: male literacy is 62%, and female literacy is 46%. In Islampur, 19% of the population is under 6 years of age.

## Jagdishpur

Jagdishpur is a city and a municipality in Bhojpur district in the Indian state of Bihar.

***Demographics:*** As of 2001 India census[GRIndia], Jagdishpur had a population of 28,071. Males constitute 52% of the population and females 48%. Jagdishpur has an average literacy rate of 50%, lower than the national average of 59.5%: male literacy is 60%, and female literacy is 40%. In Jagdishpur, 18% of the population is under 6 years of age.

## Jainagar

Jainagar is a city and a notified area in Madhubani district in the Indian state of Bihar.

***Geography:*** Jainagar is located at 25.05° N 84.08° E. It has an average elevation of 79 metres (259 feet).

***Demographics:*** As of 2001 India census[GRIndia], Jainagar had a population of 19,493. Males constitute 53% of the population and females 47%. Jainagar has an average literacy rate of 58%, lower than the national average of 59.5%: male literacy is 67%, and female literacy is 48%. In Jainagar, 16% of the population is under 6 years of age.

## Jamhaur

Jamhaur is a city and a notified area in Aurangabad district in the Indian state of Bihar.

***Demographics:*** As of 2001 India census[GRIndia], Jamhaur had a population of 8575. Males constitute 52% of the population and females 48%. Jamhaur has an average literacy rate of 50%, lower than the national average of 59.5%: male literacy is 60%, and female literacy is 38%. In Jamhaur, 18% of the population is under 6 years of age.

## Jamui

Jamui is a city and a municipality in Jamui district in the Indian state of Bihar. It is the district headquarters of Jamui district.

***Geography:*** Jamui is located at 24.92° N 86.22° E. It has an average elevation of 78 metres (255 feet).

***Demographics:*** As of 2001 India census[GRIndia], Jamui had a population of 66,752. Males constitute 53% of the population and females 47%. Jamui has an average literacy rate of 55%, lower than the national average of 59.5%: male literacy is 65%, and female literacy is 44%. In Jamui, 17% of the population is under 6 years of age.

## Adsar

Adsar is a very good village. People are very friendly here. Its geographical condition is excelent between jamui and adsar distance only 9KM. There is a very historical mosque there. Different types of religion resides there.

# 8

# Population and Religion

## POPULATION OF BIHAR

Bihar is a state situated in the Eastern part of India and it is the twelfth greatest state of India. It is additionally the third biggest state in the country as far as population is concerned. It is in like manner bordering with Uttar Pradesh and Jharkhand toward the south. On November 15, 2000, South Bihar was partitioned to outline the new province of Jharkhand.

As per the 2011 Census, the state was the third most crowded state in India with aggregate population of 104,099,452. Almost 89% of its population lived in provincial regions. Just about 58% of Bihar's population was underneath 25 years age, which is the highest in the country.

Talking about population, in order to check out the population of Bihar in 2018, we need to have a look at the population of the past 5 years. They are as per the following:

1. 2013 – 106 Million
2. 2014 – 107 Million
3. 2015 – 107.5 Million
4. 2016 – 108.1 Million
5. 2017 – 108.92 Million

Predicting the 2018 population of Bihar is not easy but we

can get the idea after analysing the population from the year 2013 – 17. As we have seen that every year the population increases by approximate 0.584 Million people. Hence, the population of Bihar in 2018 is forecast to be 108.92 Million + 0.584 Million = 109.504 Million. So, the population of Bihar in the year 2018 as per estimated data is 109.504 Million.

## DEMOGRAPHICS

After the 2011 Census, Bihar was the third most populous state of India with total population of 104,099,452 (54,278,157 male and 49,821,295 female). Nearly 89% of Bihar's population lived in rural areas.

The density was 1,106. The sex ratio was 918 females per 1000 males. Almost 58% of Bihar's population was below 25 years age, which is the highest in India. Most of Bihar's population belongs to Indo-Aryan-speaking ethnic groups along with few Dravidian-speaking and Austroasiatic-speaking people mostly in Chhotanagpur Plateau (now part of Jharkhand). It also attracted Punjabi Hindu refugees during the Partition of British India in 1947. Bihar has a total literacy rate of 63.82% (75.7% for males and 53% for females), recording a growth of 20% in female literacy over the period of a decade.

At 11.3%, Bihar has the second lowest urbanisation rate in India. As of the 2011 census, population density surpassed 1,000 per square kilometre, making Bihar India's most densely-populated state, but still lower than West Java or Banten of Indonesia.

According to the 2011 census, 82.7% of Bihar's population practised Hinduism, while 16.9% followed Islam.

## GROWTH RATE OF POPULATION IN DISTRICTS

The population of a country or its constituent states keep changing over a period of time. The excess of incidence of births over that of deaths causes an increase in the population of the country or the state and this is termed as natural increase. Migration is another important factor for population variation, though, normally it does not have a substantial effect on the population growth of any country or state. Hence, it is mainly the interaction of births and deaths that alters the population status of any country or state.

The diagram depicting the decennial growth rate (1901-2001) of Bihar is presented in this paper. It is observed from Table that the growth rate has shown very wide fluctuations in the districts over the decades.

During 1901-11, while the state and most of its districts have shown an increase in growth rate of their population, the districts of Patna, Nalanda, Bhojpur, Buxar, Kaimur, Rohtas, Saran, Siwan and Gopalganj have shown a decrease in their population size although the decrease has been very nominal in case of Patna and Nalanda.

During 1911-21, when the population of the state and most of the districts decreased, there was an increase in population in Saran, Siwan, Gopalganj, West Champaran, East Champaran, Purnia, Katihar, Araria and Kishanganj districts of north Bihar.

From the decade 1921-31 onwards, no district in the state registered a negative growth rate, i.e. decline in population, although fluctuations were noticed in the population growth rate among the districts in all the succeeding decades.

From the decade 1951-61, almost all the districts had started showing substantial increase in the growth rate of population.

In the decade 1991-2001, as many as 22 districts have recorded population growth rate higher than the state average (28.43%) among which the newly created district of Sheohar ranks first (36.16%). The district with lowest population growth rate during the decade is Nalanda (18.64%) which, in fact, has shown a decline in the population growth rate vis-à-vis 1981-91 (21.73%).

## Sex Ratio

It has been observed during various Censuses that the number of males and females are rarely at parity, the males generally outnumbering the females. The sex-ratio, expressed as the number of females per 1000 males, indicates whether there is any deficiency or surplus of females in the population. The sex-ratio is said to be favourable to the females if the number of females exceeds that of the males, and adverse, if the opposite holds good.

As may be seen, the sex-ratio for the state has been favourable to females till 1961 except in the year 1931 when it came down to 995.

After 1961, sex ratio has always remained unfavourable to females and the general trend during this period, over the decades, is that of decreasing sex ratio with exceptions of increases in 1961 and the present Census i.e. Census of India 2001. There has been an increase of 14 points in the sex ratio of Bihar at 2001 Census (921) vis-à-vis 1991 Census (907).

The sex ratio in Bihar since 1901 had always remained higher than that for the country as a whole till 1981 Census. However, the sex ratio of 911 for the composite state of Bihar and 907 of the leftover Bihar (after separation of Jharkhand) state, recorded in 1991, is much below the national sex ratio of 927.

At the Census of India 2001, sex ratio of Bihar at 921 is still lower as compared to the national sex ratio which is 933. States having higher sex ratio than that of Bihar are Kerala (1058), Chhattisgarh (990), Tamil Nadu (986), Andhra Pradesh (978), Manipur (978), Meghalaya (975), Orissa (972), Himachal Pradesh, (970), Uttaranchal (964), Karnataka (964), Goa (960), Tripura (950), West Bengal (944), Jharkhand (941), Mizoram (938), Assam (932), Rajasthan (922) and Maharashtra (922).

The state of Gujarat has recorded the same sex ratio (921) as has been observed in case of Bihar. Kerala is the only state in the country which has recorded a favourable sex ratio for females according to the provisional population figures of Census of India 2001.

It can further be seen from Table placed at Annexure-3 that Gopalganj, Siwan, Saran and Nawada are the four districts where sex-ratio had always remained favourable to the females right from 1901 to 1981. However, Siwan has had the privilege of having a favourable sex-ratio till Census of India 2001.

There are a few districts such as Sheohar, Sitamarhi, Madhubani, Darbhanga, Muzaffarpur, Vaishali and Samastipur where a favourable sex-ratio had been an important phenomenon of population characteristics till 1961 Census but the sex-ratio has shown a declining trend thereafter.

However, according to the provisional population figures, sex-ratio has shown an upward trend during 2001 Census in all the districts of Bihar with the sole exception of Bhojpur district, where the sex-ratio has slightly declined and Vaishali district, where the sex-ratio has remained unchanged.

From the statement, it would appear that sex-ratio is favourable to females only in two districts viz, Siwan (1033) and Gopalganj (1005) during 2001 Census.

These two districts occupied the first two positions at the time of 1991 Census also, but then Gopalganj district had recorded a sex-ratio (968) of less than the parity level. While Saran and Nawada districts have also retained their position during the two Censuses, Madhubani and Kishanganj have exchanged their places.

## DENSITY OF POPULATION

Population in relation to the area is termed as population density. In this paper, the number of persons living in an area of one square kilometer has been taken as the density of population (persons/sq.km). It can be seen from Table placed at Annexure–1 that the density of population, that is, number of persons per sq. km. in Bihar is 880 during 2001 Census as against 685 at the time of 1991 Census.

After bifurcation of the state of Bihar and creation of the new state of Jharkhand, the density of this state has considerably increased, since Bihar possesses comparatively less geographical area to its share in proportion to population size, while Jharkhand state is much sparsely populated in comparison to the area that has come to its share.

This has resulted in sudden rise in population density of the left over Bihar state. Bihar now ranks second in density of population among the 28 states of the country and comes only after the state of West Bengal which has a population density of 904. All other states have lower densities in varying degrees.

## LITERACY

One of the important characteristics of the population, on which information is obtained in the census, is literacy. For the purpose of census, a person is deemed to be literate if he or she can read and write with an understanding of any language. A person who can merely read but cannot write is not considered as literate. A person could, however, be a literate without having had any formal education or having passed any minimum educational standard.

Ability to merely sign one's name is not adequate to qualify a person as literate.

In the earlier Censuses, that is, till 1971, all children of the age of 4 years and less were treated as illiterate, even if some among them attended school and had picked up reading and writing of a few odd words. However, since 1981, the population aged seven years and above is to be classified as literate or illiterate. In view of this, during 2001 Census, the question on literacy was canvassed only for population aged seven years and above.

## RELIGION

Religions in Bihar:

Hinduism (82.69%)

Islam (16.87%)

Christianity (0.12%)

Other religions (0.31%)

Hindu Goddess Sita, the consort of Lord Rama is believed to be born in Sitamarhi district in the Mithila region of modern-day Bihar.

Gautama Buddha attained Enlightenment at Bodh Gaya, a town located in the modern day district of Gaya in Bihar. Vasupujya, the 12th Jain Tirthankara was born in Champapuri, Bhagalpur.

Vardhamana Mahavira, the 24th and the last Tirthankara of Jainism, was born in Vaishaliaround the 6th century BC.

*Portrait of Goddess Sita*

*Vishnupadh Temple, Gaya, Bihar*

*Buddha's statue at Bodh Gaya's temple*

*31 feet Statue of Lord Vasupujya, Champapur, Bhagalpur*

*Sita Kund at Sitamarhi, Mithila, Bihar is believed to be the birthplace of Hindu Goddess Sita*

# 9

# Art, Architecture, Fair and Festivals

## ART AND CRAFTS

Bihar has a rich historical past. Right from the ancient history to the present century it was always a center of attention of historians. Powerful dynasty like Magadha Majanapadas, Mauryan Empire and Gupta Empire had flourished in the fertile land of Bihar. Some great name of Indian History like Ashok, Chandragupta Mauryan and the symbol of peace and non-violence Gautam Buddha had their root in Bihar. Some of the great religions of the world like Buddhism and Jainism had sprouted form here. Thus naturally Bihar is rich with varied arts and crafts. Throughout the generation the rich heritage of art and crafts has been preserved though there are slight variations due to introduction of modern technologies.

The unique features of art and crafts in Bihar are the intrinsic beauties and great creativeness. These creative beauties have been preserved in various forms like in ancient stone, wooden structures, grass-clothes, lacquer and metal-wares. Bihar's craftsmen have excelled in manufacturing artistic goods which have great demands in local and international market. The fine skill and perfection of Bihari craftsmen is clearly manifested from various archeological excavations in Kumhrar,

Bulandibagh, Nalanda and other places. Pottery, wooden articles, metal wares, stone wares, jewelry, lacquer works, kashida, sikki and moonj wares, wooden and clay toys, zari, artistic textile fabrics and printing on cloth are some of the contemporary crafts of Bihar which are known in Indian as well as international markets for their artistic beauties and innovations.

Another chief feature of Bihar's handicraft is their practicality and usefulness in everyday life like bangle making, khatwa works and stone works. However reasonable price the most important feature of the art and crafts in Bihar because of which there are in great demands in Indian as well as in foreign markets.

### *Madhubani Painting*

Madhubani paintings as the name says get its name from Mithila region of Bihar where it is widely practised particularly by women. The history of Madhubani paintings goes back to the time of Ramayana. Originally the painting was done on freshly plastered mud wall of huts, but now it is also done on cloth, hand-made paper and canvas. Madhubani painting mostly depict nature and Hindu religious figures and the themes generally associated with Hindu deities, Natural objects like sun, moon, and religious plants like tulsi.

### *Rock Paintings*

Rock paintings are a particular form of paintings done on the walls and ceilings of the cave shelter of ancient man. These paintings were the reflections of their social, cultural, religious and economic life. His main object of drawing were objects of nature like sun, moon, stars, animals, birds, plants, trees and rivers etc. Besides he used to draw several activities of everyday life like hunting, running, dancing and walking. These paintings were engraved on the walls and ceilings of the rock shelters with the help of some sharp objects like rock or metal pieces. Thereafter various indigenous colours like colours extracted form leaves of trees are applied on it.

### *Paintings*

Paintings are the reflections of various aspects of human life. It is the artistic manifestation of his social, cultural, religious and economic life. The ancient men generally drew paintings about the various event of his daily life. Indians knew the art of painting since prehistoric times. Caves of Bhimabetka and Ajanta are the milestones which Indian Painting's heritage. He uses to draw pictures of natural phenomena, trees, animals, birds, rivers, his religious beliefs and economic activities. Painting in India has come a long way since then, and today represents the influences it drew from a blend of tradition and styles like Greeco-Roman style, Persian style, Mughal style and British style.

### *Wooden Work*

From time immemorial Bihar had a history of wooden craft which consist of manufacturing of wooden furniture and toys. Right from the time of Mauryan and most particularly form the time of Ashok it has remained high on scale in terms of artistic beauties, creativity, durability and cheap price. During Ashok's reign beautiful royal throne, royal gates or doors and panels of temples were manufactured by wood artists of Bihar. This ancient and rich tradition of wood work has now converted into a big industries because of their huge demands in Indian and international markets. Patna is a very famous centre of wooden toy making. Similarly Danapur is also quite known for wooden furniture manufacturing.

### *Wood Carvings*

Wood craving as a form of art and craft was very famous during Mauryan times. During such period wooden houses were made by carving out of wood. This ancient art has not only been preserved but also has been converted into a means of livelihood by artists of Bihar which in one of the few places where wood carving work is still practiced. Bihar is one of the few places where The wood carving and inlay work is done with wall plaques, table tops, pens and paper cutters being from wood and inlaid with diverse materials ranging from metal, ivory, stag horn to chips of different wood. Presently Patna is well known for manufacturing of craved doors and windows.

### *Pottery Works*

Pottery is made on clay. Bihar had a rich history of clay pottery work. Since the time of Mauryan and Gupta this art has been in practice in Bihar. The archeological excavations at places like Nalanda and Rajgir had confirmed the existence of this artistic craft in Bihar. Beautiful earthen utensils and tiles are made by potters of Bihar. They have the abilities and skill to do artistic and beautiful paintings on earthen pots. Patna is very famous for such work. Patna is also famous for making earthen statutes of various gods and goddess.

### *Bamboo Work*

Bamboo work has been remained a culture of Bihar throughout the ages and time. Right form the pre-historic time forest dwelling tribes are experts in bamboo and cane work. They used to make many utility items like baskets, household wares, woven mats, furniture and cane products like cane furniture and other decorative objects. By utilizing their skill and techniques they turned these lifeless bamboo and cane into living object which are of great value in every day life.

### *Sikki Works*

Sikki is a grass or a weed thrived on most of the river bank. Sikki work is a craft whereby the craftsmen turned these once unnecessary riverside weed into beautiful decorative objects. This craft is particularly practiced by women artisan in Bihar. Beautiful toys and wares are manufactured out of this grass. After collecting and drying they stitch these grasses into various shapes like elephant, bird, snake and tortoise. They then put various dazzling colours on these toys to make it more attractive.

### *Brass Works*

The brass work of Bihar is a continuation of the brass craft dome in pre-historic ages. But this form of art was at its peak during Mauryan and again during Gupta and Pala period. It has been confirmed from many archeological excavation sites like Nalanda and Rajgir. Even now artists of Bihar are very skillful in making images of god/goddesses, utensils, iron pitchers and other household utility articles with great fineness.

### *Tikuli Works*

Tikuli is a form of craft made from broken glass. The craftsmen first melt the broken glass and then give is shape and design. Patna and Harihans cities are very famous for manufacturing of this craft. The chief markets of Tikuli are Banaras, Patna and Calcutta.

### *Zari Works*

Artistic embroidery and Zari works is very famous in Bihar and is also a livelihood business for many families. Some of the finest Zari works can be found in shamiyanas, kanath, chandwas, pillow-covers, batwas, covers for musical instruments, tablecloth, window curtains, blouse pieces, sari, borders, etc. Patna is very famous for Zari and embroidery works.

### *Kasida Work*

The Kasida embroidery work is a very ancient form of art. Kasida embroidery is done with gold and silver metallic threads beads, silk, and sequins on satin or velvet having the motifs of birds, leaf and many other. Kasida embroidery with geometrical patterns is very famous in Bihar. Patna is a known center of such type of Kasida embroidery.

### *Textile Printing*

Textile printing is as ancient in Bihar as other form of art and crafts. Particularly Patna is very famous for this art which is specialized for making chunris having motifs like, parrots, peacocks elephants, mangoes, conches, fish and various deities.

### *Jewelry*

Silver and gold jewellery making is really associated with the history of Bihar which was cornerstone of Indian history particularly during the ancient times. Therefore silver and gold Jewellery works are very special in Bihar. Goldsmiths of Bihar are very famous for making beautiful and artistic ornaments of gold and silver. Particularly the craving or kundan work on silver Jewellery is highly praiseworthy because it requires high degree of skill and concentration.

### *Patna Kalam*

Many Indian schools of paintings were flourished afterwards and they were heavily influenced by Mughal paintings. One among these was Patna School of Painting or Patna Kalam or Company painting. As we go back to history Patna Kalam was an offshoot of Mughal painting flourished during early 18th to mid 20th century in Bihar. Although they followed the basic features of Mughal painting their subject matter was different. Unlike Mughal painting whose subjects were mainly royalty and court scenes, painters of Patna Kalam were deeply influenced by daily life of common people. Their main subjects were bazaar scenes, local rulers, local festival and ceremonies.

### *Lacquer Works*

Bihar has a rich past of highly artistic and beautiful lacquer ware craft. Bihar's lacquer ware artisans are very famous for decorating various items beautifully with lacquer ware work like legs of beds, boxes, bangles and stools. Muzaffarpur, Darbhanga and Madhubani are famous for the lacquer-work, especially for production of lac-bangles.

## MAURYAN PILLARS & SCULPTURES

The Lion-crowned pillar, Lauriya, Namdangarh in Champaran, is the finest monolithic pillars of Ashoka. It consists of a polished block of sandstone 10.1 meters long with a capital nearly 2.13 meters in length. Two other inscribed pillars are found at Rampurwa and Laurya at Basark. All four were set up on the imperial road from Pataliputra to Nepal. The edicts of the emperor are inscribed on rock at the Dhauli Hill in Orissa and on a hill near Sasaram in Bihar.

Buddhistic statuary in the Gaya district is the only class of Indian Buddhist art that has come down through ages in a fair state of completeness. At Bodh Gaya, the oldest Buddhist memorial (55 meters high temple) is a stone railing ornamented with friezes, panels and bosses, that shows considerable artistic skill. The stupa was originally a copy in brick or stone of an earthen sepulchral tumulus and ending with the ornamented spire of the medieval period.

### *Islamic Architecture*

Islamic architecture has Minar domes, vaults and arches with an exclusive use of mortar and concrete. A typical architectural splendor is the mausoleum of Magdum Shah Daulat at Maner, 29 kilometers west at Patna. Hindu symbols representing elephants, bulls and lotuses also carved on its walls.

The buildings at Bankipur and Padri-ki-Haveli are constructed as per the Gothic architecture. Golghar is the site of a famous granary, built in 1786. The Sultan Palace on the Gardiner Road, Patna represents the twentieth-century Muslim architectural style.

### *Modern Era*

In the nineteenth century, Pucca (strong) houses, large in size with baked bricks, mortar, lime, molasses and timber began to be constructed. The poorer section of the people used Gilaba rather than lime and mortar and country tiles for their roofs. From about the twentieth century, cement and sand began to be used in places of mortar and lime. People began to project porticos and balconies unsupported by pillars. Construction of buildings even at marshy places became possible and gigantic structures with deep iron foundations have come up in Bihar.

### *Local Arts*

The Maithils (people of ancient Mithila) succeeded to some extent in preserving their rich art traditions. Their Brahmins,

Kayasthas and their women folk continued their traditional practices which kept alive the ordinary domestic arts of painting earthen pots and mud walls with gods and goddesses.

Bihar Government has begun to play a vital and active role in promoting cultural forms and in providing opportunities to individual and group talents. After independence, Bihar took the lead in establishing the state academy of music, dance and drama even before the National academy was set up. With the help of All India Fine Arts and Crafts society, Bihar's own Shilpakala Parishad, organized exhibitions on the regional level. Bihar was first, in organizing and holding regional festivals such as Vaishali festival. Bihari craftsmen have excelled in terracotta, bamboo-work, Seenk-work, Kasida, Pottery, stone craft, textiles etc.

## ARCHITECTURE

The first significant architectural pieces in Bihar date back to the Vedic period. While the Mauryan period marked a transition to the use of brick and stone, wood remained the material of choice. Contemporary writers, like Chanakya in the Arthashastra, advised the use of brick and stone for their durability. However, in his writings, Megasthenes described a wooden palisade encircling the capital city of Pataliputra. Evidence of ancient structures have been found in recent excavations in Kumrahar, in modern-day Patna. Remains of an 80-pillared hall have also been unearthed.

The Buddhist stupa, a dome-shaped monument, was used in India as a commemorative monument used to enshrine sacred relics. The stupa architecture was adopted in Southeast and East Asia, where it became prominent. Many stupas, like those at Nalanda and Vikramshila, were originally built as brick and masonry mounds during the reign of Ashoka (273 BCE - 232 BCE). Fortified cities with stûpas, *viharas*, and temples were constructed during the Maurya empire (c. 321–185 BCE). Wooden architecture remained popular, while rock-cut architecture became solidified. Guard rails—consisting of posts, crossbars, and a coping—became a safety feature surrounding a stupa. Upon its discovery by Westerners, the stupa became known as *pagoda* in the West.

Temples—build on elliptical, circular, quadrilateral, or apsidal plans—were constructed using brick and timber. The Indian gateway arches, the *torana*, reached East Asia with the spread of Buddhism. Some scholars hold that *torii* derives from the torana gates at the Buddhist historic site of Sanchi (3rd century BCE – 11th century CE).

Important features of the architecture during this period included walled and moated cities with large gates and multi-storied buildings, which consistently used arched windows and doors. The Indian emperor Ashoka, who ruled from 273 BCE to 232 BCE, established a chain of hospitals throughout the Mauryan empire by 230 BCE. One of the edicts of Ashoka reads: "Everywhere King Piyadasi (Ashoka) erected two kinds of hospitals, hospitals for people and hospitals for animals. Where there were no healing herbs for people and animals, he ordered that they be bought and planted."

Buddhist architecture blended with Roman and Hellenestic architecture to give rise to unique new styles, such as the Greco-Buddhist style.

Rock-cut stepwells in India date from 200–400 CE. Subsequently, the wells at Dhank (550–625 CE) and the stepped ponds at Bhinmal (850–950 CE) were constructed.

Bihar was largely in ruins when visited by Xuanzang, and suffered further damage at the hands of Mughal raiders in the 12th century. Though parts of the Bihar have been excavated, much of its ancient architecture still lies buried beneath the modern city.

Persian influence can be seen in surviving Mughal tombs made of sandstone and marble. Surviving Mughal architecture includes Sher Shah Suri Tomb, built by Sher Shah Suriand his successor. Ibrahim Khan, Governor of Bihar and a disciple of Makhdum Daulat, oversaw the completion of Makhdum Daulat mausoleum in 1616. Another example of Mughal architecture is the building at Maner Sharif. The domed building features walls adorned with intricate designs and a ceiling full of inscriptions from the Quran.

Patna High Court, Bihar Vidhan Sabha, Bihar Vidhan Parishad, Transport Bhawan, Patna, Golghar St. Mary's Church and Patna Museum are some example of Indo-SaracenicArchitectures.

Strips or cane reeds painted in vivid colors are commonly found in Bihari homes. A special container called a "pauti," woven out of Sikki Grass Craft in the north, is a sentimental gift that accompanies a bride when she leaves her home after her wedding. Bihar is well known for the games played there, for example - kabaddi. Bhagalpur is well known for its sericulture, manufacture of silk yarn, and silk-weaving. Silk produced here is called tussah or tussar silk. Appliqué works in Bihar are known as Khatwa.

## SONEPUR CATTLE FAIR

Legend apart, the famous Sonepur fair in more of a cattle trading centre where incredible number of birds and cattle are brought from different parts of the country. Besides, the bewildering array of wares are on sale and add to this the numerous folk shows about which the BBC once remarked, "there's nothing like the Sonepur Cabaret."

The time to start is very early in the morning when the fog is suddenly pierced by the sun and the huge gathering has just emerged from the holy dip in the cold absolving waters.

The mela that lasts upto a fortnight, provides enough time to talk to the parrots, watch the elephants being bathed leisurely, followed by ear splitting trumpets and then the artists working up with colourful designs to decorate the elephants as if the pachyderm has been tatooed all over, see the horses being tested for their speed and stamina, big bulky buffaloes being milked and likewise all other animals demonstrating their skill, strength and productivity. By midday, it is the cacophony of strong decibels pouring in from all corners as the huge gathering becomes denser with more and more people adding to the sound and sight of the landscae. Ash smeared, saffron clothed holy men blow their conches and bang their gongs. Loudsspeakers, from various folk shows and jugglers rent the air together with the unison from the animals.

Much before the sun sets in, flames and fumes of dung fire burning at different places appear to screen the sky in a very amusing way, as if some mediveval army has just camped for the night. and it is time to share a gossip with one of the villagers who may better summarise the stock and sale of the cattles for the day. Zesty snacks together with tea comes in from the open air restaurant.

## Nag Panchmi

The rainy month of Sravana when there is danger of death from snake bite, people appease the snake god by offering milk during Nag Panchmi. The prime centre of naga worship is Rajgir and Mahabharata describes this place as the abode of serpents and excavations have revealed numerous objects used in serpent cult. In fact naga worship is wide spread through out India.

## Makar Sankranti Mela

Famous Makar Sankranti mela is another festival unique to Rajgir in the month of Paus, corresponding to mid January. Devotees make flower offerings to the deities of the temples at Hot springs and bathe in the holy water. Another historic place associated with fifteen day long Makar Sankranti mela is the Mandar hills in Banka district. Puranic legends accounts for a great deluge which witnessed the creation of a Asura that threatened the gods.

Vishnu cut off the Asura's head and piled up the body under the weight of the Mandar hill. The famous panchjanya - the sankh (counch shell) used in the Mahabharat war is believed to have been found here on the hills. Traces, akin to serpent coil can be seen around the hill and it is believed that the snake god offered himself to be used as a rope for churning the ocean to obtain the amrit (nectar).

## Hari Har Dham

At Bagodar in Giridih is Hari Har Dham, famous for the 62 feet high linga (completed in 1987), which marks it as the tallest in the world. Spread over 25 acres of land and surrounded by rivers, the place offers a picturesque surrounding.

## Gaya-Buddhist Pilgrimage Centre

Gaya is another holy dot in Bihar, famous for the International Buddhist Gathering and the rallying point is the Mahabodhi tree and the adjacent temple. The occasions are Buddha Jayanti (Buddha was born on this day, he attained enlightenment on this day and also attained Nirvana on this day ) and in the month of Vaisakh (April/May) and the annual session of Dalai Lama in December. Mahavir Jayanti is celebated in April with much fanfare on the Parsvanath hill and also at Vaishali while Deo Deepawali, marking the attainment of Nirvana by Mahavira is celebrated best at Pawapuri, ten days after Deepavali.

## Gaya - Pitrapaksha Mela

Arond september the sleepy town of Gaya is agog with people who come here for the famous Pitrapaksha mela or the ancestor worship typified in Sraddha ritual. It is time for the Gayalis (the descendants of Magga Brahmans who were once devotees of Shiva but later converted to Vaishnavism) to be prepared for the vedic Sraddha ceremonies or the pindan - a mandatory Hind rite that is supposed to bring salvation to the departed soul.

In the early Dharmasastras, Vishnu provides a list of over 50 tirthas but it proclaims that dead ancestors pray to God for a son who would offer pinda (lymph of rice) to them at Gaya.

The tradition traces its history to the time of Buddha, who is believed to have performed the first pindan here. Turning the pages of earlier history, one comes across the Puranic legend that ascribes Gaya as one of the holiest spots of the world. The Asura, named Gaya become so powerful that the gods felt threatened and thus thought of eliminating him. As a precondition to his death, the Asura demanded that be should be buried in the holiest spot of the world. This place is Gaya.

## Vishnupada Temple

The central point of the Hindu pilgrimage in Gaya is the Vishnupada temple built by Rani Ahilyabai of Indore in 1787. The spot on which it stands is associated with the famous mythological event of Vishnu killing Gaya and leaving his footprints on the rock which is the main point of worship in the temple.

The Shraddha is customarily performed under a fig tree while the women pilgrim perform it indoors as gayawal women live under strange customs, for instance, they never stir out of the house, married girl continues to get her daily ration from her parents. They can adopt a child or even an adult, who may assist her in their work. The Gayawals are believed to maintain centuries old records of the pindans performed under the supervision of their ancestors and accordingly people prefer the specific family of Gayawals who might have served their ancestors as well.

# FESTIVALS OF BIHAR

India has had a tradition of festivals from time immemorial. From national festivals to social ones, people come closer, enjoy and forget their differences. Festivals always break the monotony of day-to-day life and inspire us to promote love and brotherhood and to work for the upliftment of the society. Bihar as a part of this ancient land is no exception and has a long list of celebrations.

## Chatth Puja

Almost all civilizations have worshipped the 'sun god', but it has a unique form in Bihar. Chatth Puja is the only occasion where the setting sun is worshipped.The people of Bihar have immense faith in this festival. It is celebrated twice a year. Once in Chaitra (according to the Hindu calendar) which falls in March and in Kartik which falls in November. For this 4-day festival, people maintain sanctity and purity from even a month ahead. People celebrate this festival with immense faith the folk songs sung in the honour of 'Surya Dev' and 'Chatti Maiyya' can be heard at every nook and corner the sweetness of the songs lets you feel the holiness of the festival.

Women fast for the good of their family and the society. Regardless of the social status, to celebrate this festival only the faith counts. Though it is a festival of the Hindus, some of the Muslims also participate actively in the puja.

## Sama-Chakeva

It is during the winter season that the birds from the Himalayas migrate towards the plains. With the advent of these colourful birds, celebration of sama–chakeva is done. This is a festival especially celebrated in mithila. mithilanchal dedicates this festival to the celebration of the brother sister relationship.

It represents the tradition of this land as well as the art of making idols. This festival starts with the welcoming of the pair of birds sama-chakeva. Girls make clay idols of various birds and decorate them in their own traditional ways.

Various rituals are performed and the festival joyfully ended with the 'vidai' of sama and with a wish that these birds return to this land the next year.

## Ramnavami

A Hindu festival celebrated in all parts of the country. This is the auspicious day when lord RAMA was born. People celebrate it observing fasts and offering prayers in his honour.

## Makar-Sankranti

Also known as Tila Sankranti, the festival marks the beginning of the summer season. People believe that from this day on, the days become longer and the heat of the sun also increases. Every year it is observed on the 14th of January. People celebrate it by giving offerings to the poor.

## Bihula

Bihula is a prominent festival of eastern Bihar especially famous in Bhagalpur district. There are many myths related to this festival. People pray to goddess Mansa for the welfare of their family.

## Madhushravani

This festival is celebrated all over mithilanchal with much enthusiasm. It is celebrated in the month of Sawan (Hindu calendar), which falls around August. This festival carries a message with itself. It teaches how to weave together religion and tradition in day-to-day life.

Basant Panchami, Shivratri, Raksha Bandhan, Holi, Durga Puja, Deepawali, Id, Bakrid, Christmas and many more festivals however big or small are celebrated with enthusiasm all over this landmass.

# OTHER FAMOUS FESTIVITIES

Though Bihar is in league with festivals like Holi, Dussehra, Deepavali but chaath puja (6 days after Deepavali) is Bihar's prime festival honouring the sun god. Unlike the zestful Holi or the expensive Deepavali) Chaath is a festival of prayer and propitiation observed with solemnity.

It is an expression of thanks giving and seeking the blessings from the forces of nature, prominent among them being the Sun and river. The belief is that a devotee's desire is always fulfilled during Chaath. Simultaneously an element of fear is alive among the devotees who dread the punishment for any misdeed during Chaath. The city remains safe during this time when criminals too prefer to be a part of the good.

## Chaath-Fasting

Chaath in Bihar can best be seen at Deo in Aurangabad or Baragaon near Nalanda, noted for their sun temples. Unlike other sun temples in India that faces East, the temple at Deo faces west and during the festival time it is the most crowded place. It is strange to see a Brahmin standing in the river water next to a Harijan! The festival is more of a sacrifice which entails purificatory preparation.

It can be performed by men or women, irrespective to caste or creed. Chaath commences with the end of Deepavali when the house is thoroughly cleaned, family members go in for a holy dip, strict saltless vegetarian menu is observed (even onions and garlic are considered unwanted during the entire festival period), all earthen vessels are reserved for the period only and all possible purity of food is adhered to; clothes have to be unstitched and people sleep on the floor.

The person observing the Chaath (known as Parvati) observes dawn to dusk fast which concludes with sweets. This is followed by another fast for 36 hours till the dawn of the final day when puja commences at the river bank much before sunrise.

The disciplined parvatis remain in water from late midnight until the ray of dawn streaks the horizons. The river is now flooded with offerings to the sun which is followed by breakfast and distribution among the gatherings.

## Mithila- Marriage Market

What once used to be the debating ground scholars debating ground in Mithila has now become saurath Sabha or the Mithila marriage market near Madhubani.

In the summer of June, Mithila Brahmins prefer to gather in the vast mango grove (thanks to the Raja, Raghav Singh, the Mithila ruler of Darbhanga for gifting the land for the ever gathering crowd of Mithila matchmakers) in the village of Surath to explore the possibilites, discuss horoscope and finally to negotiate marriages within the community but atleast five generations beyond the family.

The girl's father is on the move trying to locate a prospective bridegroom and so in the Ghatak (middleman), all the more serious to earn commissions on marriage fixtures. Once the prospective families pass through the ordeal of question session and feel satisfied by the initial scrutiny of the horoscopes, they move on to the Panjikar (registrars) who verifies the records and credentials to ensure that matrimontial alliance was not being performed within the prohibited degrees (within the seventh generation on paternal side and the fifth on the maternal side). His satisfaction earns a talpatra (palm leaf certificate) marked in red symbolising 'no objection certificate' which permits the families to establish matrimonial alliance.

The Panjikar too receives a token and he blesses the girl's father, " May your daughter bathe in milk and bear many sons." The successful families finally call off the day with a visit to the nearby Shiva temple.

The people of Mithila are believed to have followed the Panji Prabhadha (system of recorded genealogy) since the fourteenth century. These records were maintained by the Panjikars, who were later to examine the validity and purity of marriage settlements. In fact one was supposed to be are of his ancestors names and a daily rite of Tarpan ensured that people offered oblations of water in the name of each ancestor upto six or seven generations. If one recalls the name of one's acestors daily, one can not forget their names!

## Sarhul Festivals

Sarhul is the most important festival for the tribals of Chotanagpur. It is celebrated with the advent of spring (February/March) when the sal tree is full bloom. These trees in the sacred grove are highly venerated and the festival centres around the holy spirits that dwell here. The focal point of the festival is to obtain a good harvest and hence appeasement of goddess of nature.

Makar Sankranti Paus Mid January

Sarhul Chait March/April

Holi Fagun February/March

Mahavir Jayanti Vaisakh April/May

Buddha Jayanti Vaisakh April/ May

Deogarh Pilgrimage Shrawan July/August

Nag Panchmi Shrawan July/August

Pitrapaksh Mela Bhado September/October

Sonepur Cattle Fair Kartik October/November

Deepavali Kartik October/November

Chaath Kartik 6 days after Deepavali

Deo Deepavali Aghahan 10 days after Deepavali

Buddhist congregation

(dalai Lama's session) December

Rakhi Purnamasi Shrawan July/August

Shiva Ratri Fagun February.

# 10

# Education

## INTRODUCTION

Historically, Bihar has been a major centre of learning, home to the ancient universities of Nalanda (established in 450 CE), Odantapurâ(established in 550CE) and Vikramashila (established in 783 CE). This tradition of learning may have been stultified during the period of Turkic invasions, c. 1000 CE, at which point it is believed major education centres, maintained by reclusive communities of Buddhist monks removed from the local populace, were suppressed by the Turkic raids originating from central Asia .

*Front view of administrative building of IIT Patna*

Bihar saw a revival of its education system during the later part of the British rule, when Patna University, the seventh oldest university of the Indian subcontinent, was established in 1917. Some other centres of high learning established under

British rule are Patna College(established 1839), Bihar School of Engineering (1900; now known as National Institute of Technology, Patna), Prince of Wales Medical College (1925; now Patna Medical College and Hospital), Science College, Patna (1928), and Patna Women's College, among others.

A recent survey by Pratham rated the receptivity of Bihari children to their teaching as being better than those in other states.

Bihar is striving to increase female literacy, now at 53.3%, as the government establishes educational institutions. At the time of independence, women's literacy in Bihar was 4.22%.

Bihar has a National Institute of Technology (NIT) and an Indian Institute of Technology (IIT) in Patna. The National Employability Report of Engineering Graduates, 2014 puts graduates from Bihar in the top 25 percent of the country, and rating Bihar as one of the three top states at producing engineering graduates in terms of quality and employability.

As of December 2013, there are seven government engineering colleges in the public sector, and 12 engineering colleges in the private sector, in Bihar, besides government-aided BIT Patna and Women's Institute of Technology, Darbhanga. The overall annual intake of students of these technical institutes in Bihar is only 6,200.

In Bihar, government colleges are located at Muzaffarpur, Bhagalpur, Gaya, Darbhanga, Motihari, Nalanda, and Saran (Chhapra). All institutes are recognised by All India Council for Technical Education (AICTE), affiliated with Aryabhatta Knowledge University (AKU). As it is, the foundation stone of the eighth engineering college of the state government, Ramdhari Singh Dinkar Engineering College, was laid on 22 December 2013 at Begusarai, while the process of creating the infrastructure for two new engineering colleges – one each at Madhepura and Sitamarhi – has started.

NIT Patna is the second oldest engineering college of India. Its origin can be traced to 1886, with the establishment of a survey training school, subsequently renamed Bihar College of Engineering in 1932. In 2004, the government of India upgraded the college to National Institute of Technology (NIT) status. In 2007, NIT Patna was granted Institute of National Importance status, in accordance with the National Institutes of Technology Act, 2007.

*NIT Patna main building*

Bihar established several new educational institutes between 2006 and 2008. BIT Mesra started its Patna extension centre in September 2006. On 8 August 2008, Indian Institutes of Technology Patna was inaugurated with students from all over India In 2008, NSIT opened its new college in Bihta, which is now emerging as an education hub. BCE, Bhagalpur, MIT, Muzaffarpur, and the National Institute of Pharmaceutical Education and Research, Hajipur (NIPER) are in Bihar. On 4 August 2008, National Institute of Fashion Technology Patna was established as the ninth such institute in India. Chanakya National Law University and Chandragupt Institute of Managementwere established in the later half of 2008. Steps are being taken to revive the ancient Nalanda Mahavihara as Nalanda International University. Countries such as Japan, Korea, and China have also taken initiatives. The Aryabhatt Knowledge University in Patna is a centre with which all the engineering and medical colleges in Bihar are affiliated. The A.N. Sinha Institute of Social Studies is a premier research institute in the state.

Bihar e-Governance Services & Technologies (BeST) and the Government of Bihar have initiated a unique program to establish a centre of excellence called Bihar Knowledge Center, a finishing school to equip students with the latest skills and customised short-term training programs at an affordable cost. The centre aims to attract the youth of the state to improve their technical, professional, and soft skills, to meet the current requirements of the industrial job market.

Bihar has the Central Institute of Plastic Engineering & Technology (CIPET) and the Institute of Hotel Management (a central government unit) in Hajipur.

The Central University of Bihar (CUB) is one of the sixteen central universities newly established by the Government of India under the Central Universities Act, 2009 (Section 25 of 2009). The university is temporarily located on the premises of the Birla Institute of Technology, Patna. The university is likely to be relocated to Panchanpur, approximately 10 kilometres (6.2 mi) from Gaya, on 300 acres (120 ha) of land to be transferred soon from the military. On 28 February 2014, Lok Sabha Speaker Meira Kumar laid the foundation stone.

Mahatma Gandhi Central University—also established under the Central Universities Act, and Amendment Act of 2014—is situated in Motihari, the district headquarters of East Champaran district.

The All India Institute of Medical Sciences, Patna was established in 2012. It is affiliated with AIIMS, New Delhi.

Nalanda University was re-established in 2014.

The Indian Institute of Management Bodh Gaya was established in 2015.

## UNIVERSITIES

Patna University, Patna.

Chanakya National Law University, Patna.

Magadha University, Bodh Gaya.

Baba Saheb Bhim Rao Ambedkar Bihar University, Muzaffarpur.

Tilka Manjhi, Bhagalpur University, Bhagalpur.

Lalit Narayan Mithila University, Darbhanga.

Kameshwar Singh Darbhanga Sanskrit University, Darbhanga.

Jaiprakash University, Chapra.

Bhupendra Narayan Mandal University, Madhepura.

Vir Kunwar Singh University, Arrah.

Nalanda Open University, Patna.

Mazrul Haque Arabi-Farsi University, Patna.

Rajendra Agriculture University, Pusa.

### Engineering Colleges

Bihar College of Engineering (Approved by AICTE, New Delhi), Patna University, Patna - 800 005.

Bhagalpur College of Engineering (Affiliated to Tilka Manjhi Bhagalpur University), Sabour, Bhagalpur - 813 210.

Bihar Institute of Silk and Textile, Bhagalpur, Bihar.

College of Agricultural Engineering, Rajendra Agriculture University, Pusa, Samastipur - 848 125.

Maulana Azad College of Engineering & Technology (Affiliated to Magadha University and approved by AICTE, New Delhi), Anisabad, Patna - 800 002.

Muzaffarpur Institute of Technology, Muzaffarpur - 842003.

Sanjay Gandhi Institute of Dairy Technology, Rajendra Agriculture University, P.O. - Dhelwan, Lohiyanagar, Patna - 800 020.

R. P. Sharma Institute of Technology (Affiliated to Magadha University and approved by AICTE, New Delhi), West of Canal Bailey Road, Patna - 800 024.

## Management Institutions

L.N.Mishra Institute of Economic Development and Social Changes, Patna.

Gaya College (Affiliated to Magadha University), Gaya, Bihar.

Indian Institute of Business Management (Recognised by AICTE, New Delhi), Buddh Marg, Patna - 800 001.

Patna Women's College (Affiliated to Patna University), Bailey Road, Patna.

Shanti Sewa Samiti's Indian Institute of Hotel Management, 11 IAS Colony, Kidwaipuri, Patna - 800 001.

## Medical Colleges

Darbhanga Medical College, Laheriasarai.

Shree Krishna Medical College, Muzaffarpur.

Patna Medical College, Patna.

Jawaharlal Nehru Medical College, Bhagalpur.

A. N. Magadha Medical College, Gaya.

Nalanda Medical College, Patna.

Katihar Medical College, Katihar.

Mata Gujri Medical College, Kishanganj.

## Research Institutions

Central Fuel Research Institute, Jalgorda.

Rajendra Memorial Research Institute, Agamkuan, Patna.

Bihar Research Institute, Patna.

K. P. Jaiswal Research Institute, Patna.

Dr. A. N. Sinha Research Institute, Patna.

Darbhanga Research Institute, Darbhanga.

## Law Colleges

T.N.B. Law College, Bhagalpur.

S.K.J. Law College, Muzaffarpur.

A.M. College, Gaya.

Maharaja College, Arrah, Bojpur.

Patna Law College, Patna.

Bidheh Law College, Madhubani.

Law College, Samastipur.

Shivanand Mandal Law College, Madhepura.

M.S. College, Motihari.

## Ayurvedic Colleges

Tibbi College, Patna.

Astang Ayurvedic College, Bhagalpur.

Shiva Kumari Ayurvedic College, Begusarai.

Ayurvedic College, Patna.

Maharani Rameshwari Mahavidyalay, Darbhanga.

## Veterinary Colleges

Bihar Veterinary College, Patna.

Faculty of Veterinary Science & Animal Husbandry, Samastipur.

## Agriculture/Forestry Colleges and Universities

Bihar Agriculture College, Bhagalpur.

Tirhut College of Agriculture, Muzaffarpur.

Rajendra Agriculture University, Pusa, Samastipur.

Faculty of Forestry Science, Samastipur.

## Fine Arts Colleges

Faculty of Fine Arts and Crafts, Bhagalpur University.

Govt. College of Arts and Crafts, Patna.

## Laboratory and Research Centres

T.B. Demonstration and Training Centre, Patna.

T.B. Demonstration and Training Centre, Darbhanga.

Central Fuel Research Institute, Jalgorda.

Nav Nalanda Mahavihar, Patna.

## Other Institutions

Bihar College of Pharmacy, New Bailcy Road, Patna - 801 503.

Bihar Flying Institute, Civil Aerodrome, Patna.

Kishanganj Pharmacy College, Kishanganj - 855 107.

National Institute of Physiotherapy and Communication Disorders, PMP Bhawan, Kashi Nath Lane, East Lohanipur, Patna - 800 003.

Pataliputra College of Pharmacy, PO - Bihar Veterinary College Campus, New Bailey Road, Patna - 800 014.

R.L.S.Yadav College of Pharmacy, Reshmi Complex, Kidwaipuri, Patna - 800 002.

Netraheen Chatra Vidyalay, Bhagalpur.

Balika Mahavidyalay, Lakhisarai.

Bihar Rashtrabhasha Parishad, Patna.

Prakrit Jain Shastra Aur Ahinsa Sansthan, Vaishali.

A.N. Sinha Samaj Adhyayan Sansthan, Patna.

Madersa Ajeejeeya, Bihar Sharif, Nalanda.

Science College, Patna.

Muk Badhir Vidyalay, Patna.

## HIGHER EDUCATION

Patna has emerged as one of the major center of learning in India. Schools in Patna are either run by the state government or run by private trusts, organisations, missionaries. Government schools are affiliated with the Bihar School Examination Board and most private schools are affiliated with the ICSE, CBSE or NIOS boards. Some of the prominent old schools Patna like St. Joseph's Convent, St. Michael's High School, St. Xavier's School, were established by missionaries during the British Raj . Patna imparts education in fields like technology, medicine, management, law and fashion. Institutions of national repute have opened up in Patna increasing the opportunities in higher education in the state capital.

Colleges such as Indian Institute of Technology Patna, Birla Institute of Technology, Patna and National Institute of Technology, Patna are the prominent engineering colleges in Patna. Other colleges include the newly opened National Institute of Fashion Technology Patna and medical schools such as Indira Gandhi Institute of Medical Sciences, Patna Medical College and Hospital and Nalanda Medical College and Hospital. Anugrah Narayan College and B N College are among the best known colleges for commerce and humanities besides for a range of PG courses.

After coming to power, the Nitish Kumar led government opened the Chanakya National Law University, a national law university, Aryabhatta Knowledge University, a technological university of Bihar and a B-school called Chandragupt Institute of Management. Both these institutes have attracted students from not just within Bihar but also students from far flung states. A N Sinha Institute of Social Sciences, Rajendra Memorial Research Institute, Bihar Research Institute are the research institutes in Patna. The Patna University, the first university in Bihar, was established in 1917, and is the 7th oldest university of the Indian subcontinent. Patna also houses one of India's world-renowned libraries, the Khuda Baksh Oriental Library and the Sinha Library, which is one of the largest in the region.

As on date, there are six engineering colleges for boys and one for girls in public sector and nine others in the private sector in Bihar. The overall annual intake of these technical institutes offering engineering education to students in Bihar is merely 4,559. The process to create infrastructure for three new engineering colleges—one each at Madhepura, Begusarai and Sitamarhi—has started. Bihar government is also supposed to launch new medical college in Bihar.

## *Engineering*

Patna has emerged as a major center for engineering and civil services coaching. The major private IIT-JEE coaching institutes have opened up their branches in Bihar and this has reduced the number of students who go to, for example, Kota and Delhi for engineering/medical coaching. Engineering colleges in Bihar at present are:

### *Centre-funded Engg. Colleges*

- Indian Institutes of Technology, Patna (IIT Patna)
- National Institute of Technology, Patna (NIT Patna)

### *Govt. Engg. Colleges*

- Bakhtiyarpur college of engineering,Patna
- Bhagalpur College of Engineering, Bhagalpur
- Darbhanga College of Engineering, Darbhanga
- Gaya College of Engineering, Gaya
- Motihari College of Engineering, Motihari
- Muzaffarpur Institute of Technology, Muzaffarpur
- Nalanda College of Engineering,
- Lok Nayak Jayprakash Institute Of Technology, Chapra(Saran)

### *Private Engg. Colleges*

- Azmet Institute of Technology, Kishanganj
- BIT Mesra Extension Centre, Patna
- Central Institute of Plastics Engineering & Technology, Hajipur(CIPET)
- College of Agricultural Engg, Pusa, Samastipur
- Maulana Azad College of Engineering and Technology, Patna
- Millia Institute of Technology, Purnea

- Moti Babu Institute of Technology,Forbisganj Araria
- Netaji Subhas Institute of Technology, Patna
- Patna Sahib College of Engineering & Technology, Vaishali
- R.P. Sharma Institute of Technology, Patna
- Sanjay Gandhi Institution of Dairy Science & Technology, Patna
- Sityog Institute of Technology, Aurangabad, Bihar
- Siwan Engineering and Technical Institute, Siwan
- Vidyadaan Institute of Technology and Management(VITM), Buxar
- Vidya Vihar Institute of Technology, Purnea
- Women's Institute of Technology, Darbhanga

Other colleges in Bihar are

- Araria College Araria
- College of Arts and Crafts, Patna
- Cybotech campus,Patna
- Information Computer Training College Darbhanga
- International School of Management
- IMPACT College Patna
- Jagdam College, Chhapra
- Jai Prakash Narayan All India Institute of Medical Sciences
- Patna Women's College
- Radiance Institute of IT & Management (RIIM), Chhapra
- Rajendra College, Chhapra
- St. Xavier's College of Education
- St. Xavier's College, Patna

# Bibliography


Aggarwal, Santosh : *Three Language Formula: An Educational Problem*, New Delhi, Sian, 1991.

Ahmad, Imtiaz : *Caste and Social Stratification Among Muslims in India*, New Delhi, Manohar, 1978.

Asiachi, A.J. : *Curriculum Development for Schools*, Nairobi, Educational Research Publications, 1992.

Dandekar, R.N.: *Some Aspects of the History of Hinduism*, Radhey Shayam Press, Poona. 1967.

Drekmeier, Charles: *Kingship and Community in Early India*. Stanford Univ. Press, 1962.

Edward J. : *The Life of Buddha as Legend and History*, London, Routledge and Kegan Paul, 1927.

Elliott, J. : *Action Research for Educational Change*, Milton Keynes, Open University, 1991.

Gail Kelly : *New Approaches to Comparative Education,* Chicago, The University of Chicago Press, 1986.

Galbraith, M.W. : *Education Through Community Organizations*, San Francisco, Jossey-Bass, 1990.

Ghoshal U. N.: *A History of Indian Political Ideas*, Oxford University Press, Mumbai, 1966.

Giroux, H. : *Critical Theory and Educational Practice*, Geelong, Australia, Deakin University, 1983.

Heesterman J. C.: *Ancient Indian Royal Consecration*, E. J. Brill, The Hague, 1957.

Jayasuriya, J.E. *Education in Korea: A Third World Success Story*, Colombo, Associated Educational Publishers, 1980.

Kangle R. D.: *The Arthashastra of Kautilya*, University of Mumbai, Mumbai 1975.

Krishna Murari: *The Calukyas of Kalyani, from circa 973 A.D. to 1200 A.D.*, Delhi, Concept, 1977.

Krishna Rao M. V.; *Studies in Kautilya*, Munshiram Manoharlal, Delhi, 1979.

Macdonell, Arthur A: *Vedic Index of Names and Subjects*. London: Murray, 1912.

Majumdar, Ramesh C.: *The History and Culture of the Indian People*. London: Allen & Unwin, 1951.

Minakshi, C.: *Political History and Social Life under the Pallavas*, Madras, University of Madras, 1977.

Mookerjee R. R.: *Local Government in Ancient India*, Oxford University Press, 1920.

Possehl, Gregory L.: *The Harappan Civilization*, London, Aris and Phillips, 1982.

Prahlad K.: *Governance and Public Administration for Poverty Reduction*, Salvador, Brazil, 1997.

Prasad, Lal Bahadur : *Indian Political System and Law*, New Delhi, Shree, 2005.

Rosenblum, G.: *Law as a Political Instrument,* New York, Random House, 1955.

Shani, G.: *Communalism, Caste and Hindu Nationalism: The Violence in Gujarat*, Cambridge Univ Press, Delhi, 2003.

Simon, D. : *Public Administration,* New York, Knopf, 1950.

Sudarshan, R. : *Human Development and Structural Adjustment,* New Delhi, McMillan, 1993.

Sudarshan, R. : *Human Development and Structural Adjustment,* New Delhi, McMillan, 1993.

Uphoff, N.: *Local Organizations: Intermediaries in Rural Development*, Ithaca, Cornell University Press, 1984.

Victor G. : *Law as a Political Instrument,* New York, Random House, 1955.

Wheare, Kenneth C. : *Modern Constitutions*, New York, Oxford University Press, 1951.

Zelermyer, William (1977). *The Legal System in Operation*. St. Paul, MN: West Publishing.

# Index

❑❑❑

www.ingramcontent.com/pod-product-compliance
Ingram Content Group UK Ltd.
Pitfield, Milton Keynes, MK11 3LW, UK
UKHW042016290726
14061UKWH00001BB/20

9 789388 318686